YOU CAN CONTROL YOUR FEELINGS!

24 Guides to Emotional Well-Being

Bill Borcherdt, ACSW
Board Certified Diplomate (BCD)
in Clinical Social Work

Professional Resource Press
Sarasota, Florida

Published by Professional Resource Press
(An imprint of Professional Resource Exchange, Inc.)
Post Office Box 15560
Sarasota, FL 34277-1560

Printed in the United States of America

The copy editor for this book was Patricia Hammond, the managing editor was Debra Fink, the production coordinator was Laurie Girsch, and Jami's Graphic Design created the cover.

Library of Congress Cataloging-in-Publication Data

Borcherdt, Bill.
You can control your feelings! : 24 guides to emotional well-being / Bill Borcherdt.
p. cm.
Includes bibliographical references.
ISBN 0-943158-73-7 (pbk.)
1. Rational-emotive psychotherapy. I. Title.
RC489.R3B67 1993
158--dc20 92-46866
CIP

Dedication

To my children, Barb and Bill, who provided the reality that killed the dream - only for me to discover that reality can be more pleasant and learned than a dream.

Table of Contents

Introduction

This is a book about rational ideas that provide new ways of looking at old problems, using the principles of Rational-Emotive Therapy (RET). RET is a philosophical, educational, and therapeutic approach that emphasizes developing thoughts, feelings, and behaviors that promote happiness and survival.*

RET has a distinctive approach to problem solving that teaches you how to accept yourself more, so that you will overreact less. RET believes that unless you first take pressure off yourself for having problems, you will likely not be able to work very clearheadedly and constructively against

---

*Rational-Emotive Therapy was originated in 1955 by psychologist Albert Ellis, who is currently President of the Institute for Rational-Emotive Therapy and the Institute for Rational Living in New York City. A catalog of books and other resources is available from the Institute for Rational-Emotive Therapy, 45 East 65th Street, New York, NY 10021.

Dr. Ellis has written over 50 books about the therapy he founded, and as the grandfather of cognitive-behavior therapy, practiced by thousands of mental health professionals world wide, he has influenced the art and science of psychotherapy perhaps more than anyone who has ever lived.

This book reflects Dr. Ellis' rational teachings and writings as well as other RET therapists and writers such as Paul Hauck, PhD, Howard Young, MSW, Russell Grieger, PhD, Robert A. Harper, PhD, Michael Bernard, PhD, and Windy Dryden, PhD. Ideas presented in the book also reflect cognitive-behavioral concepts popularized by David Burns, MD, Donald Meichenbaum, PhD, Aaron Beck, MD, Michael J. Mahoney, PhD, Arnold Lazarus, PhD, and Maxie C. Maultsby, Jr., MD.

your flaws. RET respects human limitations but does not condemn people for having them; it teaches that you are not in an imperfect world to be perfect or to be perfectly comfortable, but to experience yourself and your world - including your faults and its discomforts. If you don't upset yourself by your dislikes, handicaps will not be multiplied into disabilities, and you will be more likely to achieve your higher potential.

In a direct, forthright, persuasive manner, RET presents a system of ideas for lessening the demands humans often put on themselves, others, and life. By examining and intervening in human thought in unique ways, RET doesn't claim that its clients and students will live happily ever after; rather, it helps them become more likely to live more happily and have happier relationships. Principles of rational thinking present a world view, a philosophy of living that allows you to plant the seeds of tolerance and self-acceptance so that you can reap the fruits of emotional well-being.

THE "R" IN RET

A working definition of "rational" is directly related to what humans are made of: thoughts, feelings, and behaviors. "Rational" means to more fully live, survive, and be happy; any thoughts, feelings, and behaviors that contribute to one's long-range happiness and survival can be considered to be rational.

RATIONAL THOUGHTS

The thought "I have to be perfect" would not be rational because it would likely lead to anxiety and guilt; such burdensome emotions do not lead to emotional well-being. On the other hand, the idea "I want to do well, but I am not required to do the best" is in your best interests because it permits you to be more permissive with and accepting of yourself.

RATIONAL FEELINGS

Feelings of anger, anxiety, guilt, or depression would not be in your best interests because they are likely to block you from the emotional perspective required to reach your goals. On the other hand, feelings of annoyance, apprehension, regret, and sadness will assist in producing the emotional alertness necessary to track and fine-tune your long-range objectives.

RATIONAL BEHAVIORS

Behaviors that are avoidant and procrastinating at one extreme, or aggressive and overreactive at the other, will hamper achievement of your goals. A more rational behavior would be enthusiastically moving toward your wants with an attitude of "He who doesn't hesitate will more likely find."

THE "E" IN RET

The "E" in RET represents the free-wheeling excitement that springs from new, powerful ways of looking at old problems. I can tell I'm getting through to a client when he or she says, "I never looked at it that way before." Nothing is so powerful as an idea whose time has come. RET will help you search for the truth until you find it.

RET's ways of thinking can withstand the scrutiny of scientific inquiry. It confines itself to ideas that can be supported by evidence so that you don't limit your options by holding on to unprovable notions.

Practically the only thing that RET presumes is that if you're human you have emotional cavities by nature rather than by nurture. If you had been reared on a desert island with a "perfect upbringing," you would have used your ability to disturb yourself in the same way as if you had been reared in a "dysfunctional" family. In other words, your natural tendencies to personalize, overreact, and overgeneralize would have followed you.

You may be able to run from your active part in your own emotional problems by thinking you have "special reasons" for your problems and upsets (such as being an adult child of an alcoholic parent), but you can't hide from the facts of your own fallible nature. Believing that emotional upset is due to a social or family circumstance is "barking up the wrong tree." More than any other therapy, RET holds you accountable for emotions. It holds that what emotions mainly vali- at you believe about a situation. Fortunately, any- believe you can disbelieve.

THE "T" IN RET

RET tries to better understand the human condition and rise above those tendencies that work against long-range happiness and survival. You can learn to better achieve both short- and long-range emotional well-being by practicing the ABCs of rational-emotive therapy's problem-solving structure.

Because humans are not emotional islands, they are affected by difficult circumstances at point "A" - the "activating event" (or avalanche of activating events!). Rational principles that are applied to the activating situation can be put to good use for emotional self-control in *any* future predicament to decrease overreaction and increase self-acceptance.

This is done by detecting and examining "B" (meaning "beliefs" - sometimes also used to mean blind spots, bigotry, baloney, or bullshit). It is these ideas, often not well thought out, that directly determine "C" (emotional consequences or feelings). Humans are affected by their life circumstances, but they largely create their emotional disturbance at C.

Because people mainly feel the way they think, they are capable of gaining more emotional control by thinking about their thoughts at "D" (disputing, debating) and determining that a different way of thinking about their life circumstance would get more pleasant emotional results at "E" (new effects).

Perhaps rational-emotive therapy's most basic premise is that nothing in life has to be. You don't have to be perfect, others don't have to treat you perfectly well, and the universe doesn't have to do perfectly well by you. When you not only well know, but know well, these positions, you will have taken a giant step toward achieving fuller emotional potential.

NUTRITIONAL THINKING

This book presents a menu of 24 nourishing guides for a better understanding of and coping with common problems of living using rational-emotive ideas. Some of the main ideas and finer points of rational thinking that make up the ingredients of this book are:

1. *Recognizing that not all solutions are equal.* One size *doesn't* fit all. RET clearly distinguishes high-level from low-level solutions - elegant from inelegant problem solving. Practical methods of gaining success, achievement, cooperation, approval, love, or whatever else you wish will temporarily help you to *feel better* by distracting you from your overreactions and self-downings, but such stop-gap control will not result in *getting better*. RET teaches you to heighten tolerance and self-acceptance levels, which provides for solutions that are independent of, and rise above, situational outcomes.
2. *Not presuming change.* Active disputing of mistaken notions about the problem results in inner emotional control. Some examples of active disputation are: "Where is the evidence that matters of concern should/must/have to be any different than they are?" "Where is the proof that presenting issues are awful and that I can't stand them instead of merely disliking them?" RET realistically sees that often outer problems, especially in the form of things we don't like about another's personality, don't change that much. Consequently, RET prefers to emphasize changing one's thinking about the problem so as to upset oneself less, *regardless* of whether or not the problem can be changed.
3. *Disputing the theory "If it works, use it."* What is effective (methods for making things right) may well not be efficient (in getting yourself less upset when things go wrong). Larger problems of self-evaluation and a low tolerance level for discomfort are often concealed by solutions that seem to be shortcuts but are often shortsighted.
4. *Preferring direct methods.* RET therapists tend to lead with their biases rather than long-windedly talk around them. They prefer to present direct instruction in understanding (a) how humans disturb themselves and (b) what they can quickly do to upset themselves less. Getting out on the table what's what in terms of better emotional con-

trol encourages a collaborative relationship between client and therapist.

5. *Taking issue with the theory: "The apple doesn't fall far from the tree."* RET respects individual differences and free will, believing that humans are not clones of and do not passively mirror their social or family circumstances.
6. *Distinguishing self-confidence from performance confidence.* Many have performance confidence, but few have self-confidence. Performance or achievement confidence comes from the view "I have to succeed because if I don't others would criticize me; not only would my failing and their criticisms be horrible but also it would mean I am an inferior person." Such self-statements might be a driving force behind an individual's success and may *appear* to reflect self-confidence. However, legitimate self-confidence believes "I want to succeed for the advantages success would afford me. If I don't, others might criticize my faltering, and though this would be disappointing it wouldn't be disastrous, nor would it mean that I am an inferior person." In short, self-confidence overcomes the fear of failure while performance confidence expresses it.
7. *Viewing humans as unique rather than special.* Special implies anointment, that one has been singled out for preferential treatment. This belief often tempts one to further conclude that "Because I'm so special, (a) the universe owes me special favors, (b) others are to treat me only in special ways, with no lapses in kindness and consideration, and (c) I have to always give special performances." Rational thinking encourages people to appreciate their uniqueness and their distinct ways of being in this world, but not in a way that encourages an exaggerated view of their requirements of the world.
8. *Differentiating normal from healthy.* If a certain behavior is called "normal" it simply means that most people behave that way; such behavior is not necessarily healthy. RET encourages rational nonconformity when necessary to make choices that are in your healthful best interest.

9. *Vigorously avoiding comfort traps.* RET teaches that humans don't exist in this world to feel comfortable, but rather to experience the world - and this includes some discomfort. Learning to give perspective to personal discomfort encourages an expanded lifestyle. Startling and intimidating oneself by potential discomfort will likely encourage a restrictive approach to living.
10. *Distinguishing wants from needs.* Having wants, wishes, and preferences brings motivation to life. However, insisting that these desires be met by proclaiming that you need what you want puts pressure on yourself and others. Ambitions make the world go around, but *preferring* rather than *requiring* your goals keeps you from getting dizzy.
11. *Avoiding the self-rating game and personal report cards.* RET avoids egoistic, self-proving games that result in anxiety, guilt, and depression. RET advises against the human tendency to give oneself a report card with a good or bad mark depending on how well one is performing or being accepted by others. One can avoid emotional flip-flopping by learning that no external props are required to more fully accept oneself.
12. *Seeing the therapist and client as scientists.* Using the scientific method requires gathering a data base and then proving or disproving hypotheses based on the data. In RET the therapist makes good use of scientific principles in detecting, examining, and challenging clients' belief systems. For example, a therapist may ask "Where is the proof that you have to be perfect, that others have to treat you perfectly, or that the universe has to do perfectly well by you?" Clients are encouraged to use RET as a personal science and actively and experimentally test whether their hunches about their experiences are based on fact or fiction (i.e., that failing, being rejected, or being harshly criticized would be devastating).
13. *Putting less emphasis on past happenings generally and family-of-origin material specifically.* RET believes that there is no such thing as a problem that isn't happening right now. RET defocuses on personal and family background material and refocuses on overcoming general human tendencies toward disturbance. People affect

themselves more than they are affected. They upset themselves outside their family for the same reasons they upset themselves within it. If they had not disturbed themselves in their family of origin they would have done so in a different context. The basic facts of emotional disturbance are likely to get lost when historical information is made a standard part of problem solving.

14. *Not presuming disturbance*. Emotional upset is not like the common cold; the fact that you are exposed to adverse life conditions does not mean that you will necessarily be strongly affected by them automatically and indefinitely.
15. *Distinguishing practical from emotional dependency.* The fact that you rely on someone for practical advantages (e.g., your boss to sign your checks) does not mean that you depend on that person to find value to your existence and to accept yourself. To find it desirable for someone to think well of you is one thing, but to think that if he or she does, it makes you superior, or if he or she doesn't, it makes you inferior, is quite a different thing.
16. *Encouraging independence without making it sacred.* Practically any solution carried to an extreme becomes a problem. Almighty insistence on a good thing by making yourself dependent on being independent results in reversed compulsion. "I have to be dependent" or "I have to be independent" are two different notions that create the same brand of pressure cooker.
17. *Arguing against the reverse golden rule*. Others are not required to provide an emotional refund. Treating others pleasantly is good; if they act kindly toward you in return, that is even better - but not required. Accepting others' free will to not become a clone of your conduct toward them reduces your tendency to hurtfully and angrily take others' treatment of you personally.
18. *Ripping up misery equations*. When you operate with faulty views, such as "My deficiencies equal me," "Others' opinions equal me," "My advantages equal me," or "My disadvantages equal me," you are allowing your emotional well-being to become dependent on persons and matters often beyond your control.

19. *Pointing out that what you see isn't often what you get.* Mastering a goal, winning someone's favor, or contributing to the United Fund are examples of observable behaviors that are all well and good - perhaps. If done to contribute to one's social group and/or personal happiness - yes; if done out of fear of disapproval or so as to not put yourself down if you didn't - no.
20. *Finding value in assessing for problems that don't exist.* Sadness is often mislabeled as depression; regret as guilt; irritation as anger; and apprehension as anxiety. Because humans tend to act according to how they see themselves, such emotional trademarks become self-fulfilling prophecies. RET is careful to fine-tune the anatomy of emotions so as to make clearer what the individual is up against. This can best be done by examining the belief systems that trigger emotions.
21. *Emphasizing influence by inaction.* Patience in holding your own, if not retreating, may often be the better part of valor in influencing others. Tolerance in not overreacting provides less for others to oppose, resulting in their being more likely to gravitate toward you.
22. *Identifying three things that can almost always be done.* Regardless of difficulty, humans can (a) accept themselves, (b) tolerate something, and (c) be fair to self. Developing these three forms of self-reliance makes possible the emotional security that is likely to come only from being well grounded in self.
23. *Establishing the happiness check.* RET boldly confronts the human tendency to "necessitize." Three basic questions to ask yourself are: (a) "What do I really need in life?" (not what is wanted, but what is really mandatory, required, essential), (b) "What can others really do to me?" (psychologically, not physically. Try to uncover whether there is evidence that others can discredit, humiliate, dehumanize, stigmatize, or put you down), and (c) "What does the world really owe me?"

    Rational-emotive therapy maintains that when you are able to answer all three questions with a resounding "nothing," you will create that emotion commonly described as happiness, peacefulness, or contentment.

24. *Prioritizing problem solving.* The three ways to solve a problem are to (a) remove or change the matter or person of concern, (b) distract yourself from this same circumstance or person by busying yourself with something or someone else, or (c) change your thinking about the issue. Concerning the first solution, you will find that things you dislike often cannot be changed very much, especially if they involve other humans. Regarding the second solution, you will find that avoidance provides only temporary relief. Although RET does use practical methods for distraction, it emphasizes the emotional problem-solving solution that is most accessible, most permanent, and most self-determined - changing one's thinking. Changing one's thinking about problems permit problem solvers to (a) rise above their situation by upsetting themselves less about their predicaments so that they can then either more clearheadedly problem solve or better gracefully accept what can't be changed, and (b) use this method of thought to prevent future overreactions and self-blame.

HOW TO USE THIS BOOK

Learning and practicing nourishing rational ideas will bring emotional enrichment to your life. In Addendums 1, 2, and 3 in the back of this book (pp. 223-232), you will find a digest of rational, nourishing thoughts that you can use to help you better accomplish rational-emotive therapy's goal of overreacting less and accepting yourself more. I suggest that you review these now before reading further. Identify those that seem especially advantageous to your emotional health. Transfer these to a note card or separate sheet of paper and vigorously read them over, as often as possible out loud to yourself, several times a day. This will build your emotional stamina to the point of being able to forcefully and energetically call these important nutritional thoughts to mind when you find yourself inclined to put yourself down or overreact. You can train yourself to interrupt your emotional upsets by recalling these thoughts as automatically as you can recall your telephone number or your middle initial. Each idea contains rational principles of tolerance and acceptance ready to be woven into all areas of your life. Think of how much happier you will feel as you begin to master these new ways of looking at old problems. Addendums 4 and 5 (pp. 233-239) describe some of the things to expect in the application of RET in formal psychotherapy.

Nutritional thinking provides an approach to life, not simply an approach to solving a particular problem. Its broad world view can be applied to any future concern. Nutritional thinking keeps you emotionally healthy as you grow and develop from it.

An English physician once likened ideas to food, saying that we swallow it not because of its nutritional content, but because we like it. The rational ideas described here have been found to be both likable and emotionally nourishing by my clients and students. It is my wish that you will discover them to be compatible with your growth and development also.

YOU CAN CONTROL YOUR FEELINGS!

24 Guides to Emotional Well-Being

Fact Versus Fiction: Learning to Distinguish Practical Dependency from Emotional Dependency

In the wild, the antelope startles and flees whenever it hears a twig fall. Its instincts tell it that danger, in the form of a large predator, is nearby, ready to pounce on it and devour it. Because of the antelope's instantaneous readiness to run from the presumed threat, it survives. This flight response repeatedly predominates, despite the fact that only a small percentage of these incidents is truly life-threatening. But because this animal isn't able to distinguish real from imagined danger - fact from fiction - it leads a very unsettled life.

Humans frequently conduct their lives similarly to the antelope, often feeling anxious and out of sorts due to fear of what harm they believe others can and might inflict upon them. Many people tie themselves up in knots if someone doesn't like them - or threatens not to like them. This high degree of emotional anguish might be fit for an antelope, but it is not fit or necessary for the human experience. This guide will encourage humans to do what antelopes cannot do: stop, think, and ask themselves two questions: (a) "What can others really do to me?" and (b) "What do I have to have, that I must depend on others to give me?" Accurate answers to these two questions help distinguish between real and imagined danger.

We live in an interdependent society. We depend on others for practical advantages (e.g., the boss signs the paycheck; the teacher supplies grades required for graduation; the case aide provides food stamps; physicians give medical advice). These dependencies are facts of life. The fiction begins with emotional dependencies, such as the belief that we must depend on others to assign value to ourself, or the belief that others can harm us psychologically. This imagined indebtedness often blocks a more free-spirited approach to living. Practical dependency and emotional dependency are different, and they are not inseparable. You *can* have one without the other.

Perhaps the biggest human fear is of other humans, and what these others might do to them. All right then, let's examine the facts. Besides outright physical injury, what harm can one human inflict upon another? When others withhold conveniences from us (e.g., paychecks, course grades, food stamps, advice) we may feel frustration, deprivation, inconvenience, and dissatisfaction at a practical level. However, these actions are not emotionally damaging; there is no proof to the commonly held notion that one person can disgrace, humiliate, or discredit another.

To more thoroughly unharness yourself from this fictional from-one-dehuman-to-another theory, you can challenge and uproot your personal philosophy about others' ability to upset you. You can rethink what others' likes or dislikes, appreciations or depreciations, favors or disfavors, and fairness or unfairness toward you really mean.

The following statements contrast interdependent and independent ways of thinking with dependent ways. Incorporate these in approaching your relationships with others. Test your mastery of them, and find out for yourself how they can contribute to your personal and interpersonal happiness:

- "Wanting others to think well of me helps make my world go around in that it shows my social group that their opinions are important. But making myself dependent on their liking me, by thinking that their doing so is sacred, only results in my getting myself dizzy."
- "It's best for me to appreciate others' favorable review of me as being nice and important, lest I approach my rela-

tionships with others in a casual, uncaring manner. Better that I not go beyond my desire for a favorable estimation by foolishly thinking of it as necessary and all-important."

- "Because I am not perfect, there will be times when I will wrongly make myself emotionally dependent on someone else. It's best for me to see that this is bad and acknowledge disappointment in my clinging behavior, so that I will try not to repeat such stupidity so often in my future. But this does not mean that I am bad or stupid. I would be wise not to damn myself for my slip-up as this would definitely not help my emotional cause nor assist in making fewer errors in the future. Come to think of it, there is no cosmic declaration that says I ever have to condemn myself for anything!"
- "It's good that I deliberately put my best foot forward and encourage others to draw closer to me. It's bad that I desperately fall all over myself by pleading my case as if I require that others accept me."
- "Caring less (without becoming uncaring) about what others think of me makes for a good balance as I rub elbows with my social group. Consuming myself about my concerns about how others might be taking to me results in an out-of-balance social arrangement and my feeling out of sorts!"
- "Accommodating those around me helps us to be more accessible to one another. Catering to others is likely to wear thin with me getting the short end of the stick as others begin to take me for granted. This is likely to result in hurt, anger, and self-pity - all things I need 'like a sore thumb.' "
- "Others can disapprove of me but not discredit me; they can dislike me but not diminish me; they can criticize me but not insult me; they can deprive me but not destroy me; they can select against me but not stigmatize me. Such unwanted experiences would be disappointing but not disastrous; hassles but not horrors; annoying but not intolerable; sad but not tragic."
- "Succeeding in gaining another's hoped-for approval is a pleasant part of life; failing to do so is a disappointing part of life - but not bigger than life."

- "Wanting, hoping for, and preferring another's acceptance and approval leaves a margin for error and allows me comfort and independence. Needing, requiring, or insisting on the same things results in my being uncomfortably dependent."

As you begin to more fully convince yourself of the preceding declarations, push yourself further; pick up the beat of the action component of this project toward more emotional independence. Consider these extension-of-self suggestions:

1. *Do things alone that you normally do with others.* Go to a movie, take a long bike ride, go to a bar with the company of yourself. Actively establish yourself as an enjoying person in your own right while appreciating the value and advantages of solitude.
2. *Don't let others do for you what you can and best do for yourself.* Convenient as it may be, don't allow others to wipe your nose for you. Allowing such pampering from others easily becomes habit forming, hampering learning self-initiative.
3. *View trying as habit forming.* Efforts on your own behalf have a life of their own and can be established as a routine lifestyle pattern.
4. *Avoid "the self-fulfilling prophecy."* Replace "I've never done this before and could never do it now" with "Up until now I haven't done it but perhaps there's a first time for everything." This creates the potential for change in the direction of self-initiative.
5. *Use independent speech.* "I" statements and "you" questions give practice in self-expression while solicitating ideas from others. "I think such-and-such about that; what do you think?" is a pattern that gets position statements from both sides out on the table.
6. *Avoid dependent words.* "I might," "Maybe I will," "I probably will," "Yes I'll do it, but . . ." are phrases that depend on uncertain provisions. Set them aside in favor of self-choosing phrases, without qualification.
7. *Experiment with leadership roles.* Don't wait for George to do it. In your social and family groups volunteer to

take on responsibilities that you previously have relied on others to fulfill.

8. *Teach others.* Read a self-help article or book and explain its contents to others. One of the best ways to learn or relearn something is to teach it.
9. *Try being your own best counselor.* Rather than quickly turning to someone for advice about a problem or decision, brainstorm options with yourself. Test your self-generated suggestions and see if you can better establish yourself as an independent problem solver.
10. *Organize your time better.* Take better control over your own life by better managing your time. Write down each day what you can realistically accomplish. Try to complete each of the day's tasks before going on to the next one. That way projects won't run into each other and you will avoid doing a little bit of a lot of things but not too much of any one thing.
11. *Learn a new hobby or master a new skill.* Strike out on your own; sink your teeth into a new special interest.
12. *Work against fear of the unknown.* People often act dependent because of their fear of unknown quantities that lie ahead. Try to understand that what "might be" often seems bigger than life, but once you experience it, it will simply become a part of life.
13. *Be aware of and work against fears of discomfort.* Acknowledge the queasiness, apprehension, and awkwardness that often accompany a new step in the right independent direction, but don't intimidate yourself by such feelings. Remember, you're not in the world to feel comfortable, but to experience the world - and the world includes a fair amount of discomfort.
14. *Purposefully disagree with prevailing wisdom.* Voicing your opinion when it contrasts with others' positions provides good practice in unshackling yourself from emotionally dependent bonds. Such direct expression acts against your dependency on others' approval.
15. *Affirm your strengths.* Rather than wait for others to notice your favorable traits and deeds, prove that you can always rely on yourself for the appreciation that you have made yourself dependent on others for.

16. *Solicit others' disapproval.* Actively request a critical appraisal of your performances and accomplishments. By soliciting constructive criticism (i.e., "What are some things that you think I could have done differently or better?"), you will likely develop more of an emotional immunity to others' critical comments that you had previously experienced as shattering.
17. *Notice others and think of your own independent actions.* Observe in others the self-direction you wish to develop. Think of times past when you were willing to put yourself out on an independent limb. Strongly call to mind these times that you have put your self-directed potential to good use, while fully appreciating the advantages of such emotional liberation.

Facts of life make you aware of what you're up against. Fictions leave you groping in the dark, afraid of your own emotional shadow. The next time you hear a twig drop in your life, stop and remind yourself that, like the antelope, you can run - but you can't hide. What you *can* do is rise above, set yourself apart from others' views, and more fully appreciate and enjoy what emotional self-reliance means for you. By distinguishing real from imagined danger, you will lead yourself beyond merely surviving to living more fully and being happier. What could be a better fact of life than that?

Unmasking the Mystery Emotion: Hurt as Self-Blame and Self-Pity

Hurt is perhaps the most silent and most crippling feeling state in the human experience. Feeling hurt takes the wind out of our motivational sails. Hurt is a helpless, weak, empty feeling that saps energy and effort. Often we aren't aware of where it comes from, and not being able to put a finger on its source often is followed by making ourself feel further weakened and distraught. Frequently hurt is quickly transformed into anger (e.g., "You hurt me, you bastard!"). But little attention is given to uncovering its beginnings.

Like all emotions, hurt is created and maintained by one's belief system. Finding and uprooting the faulty ideas allows one to get past the disguises of hurt and get on with the rest of one's life more energetically. This guide will (a) provide a technical, organized understanding of how hurt is created and maintained and (b) review the means by which boundaries for curtailing this burdensome response can be set.

"Sticks and stones may break my bones, but words will never hurt me." How often we hear this popular phrase! But it would be better to continue: ". . . words will never hurt me *unless I sharpen them up and stick them in myself.*" Simply put, hurt is self-inflicted; it is created by self-blame and/or self-pity. Hurt takes a handicapping remark from someone else and turns it into a personal emotional disability. If you are determined not to put yourself down or feel sorry for yourself in spite of another's ill-advised treatment of you, you will be hard put to feel hurt. For instance, if someone you feel close to unfairly criticizes you, and you begin to feel a gnawing in your gut, don't assume that it is the unkind comments that are causing your emotional pain. Rather, examine what these comments mean to you. It is your interpretation of the person's comments that is rattling your emotional cage, not the comments themselves.

The diagram on pages 12 and 13, entitled "The Anatomy of Hurt, Part I" illustrates rational-emotive therapy's ABCs of emotional reeducation as applied to this often-camouflaged emotion. Part II (pp. 14-15) illustrates how, once the hurt is established, it often becomes the "A" (the activating event) when it is transformed into anger. Frequently, false conclusions about hurt bring on the more visible feelings of anger; because anger is a more potent, energetic feeling, it is often quickly substituted for the less lifelike hurt. Hurt often "suffers in silence," while anger often intends to cause the other to suffer.

Changing your beliefs will clear up your distorted view of the situation and your personalized overreaction to it. First, realize that your associate didn't cause your hurt to begin with; your false assumptions did. Then, accept the original facts of the matter; namely, that your associate's unkind manner does not represent you but rather his or her unhappy state of mind at the time the accusations were made.

Smoke out the hurt. Examine it for what it is - rooted in self-blame and self-pity, and often used as a springboard toward anger. Then, consider the following suggestions in an effort to diminish its happiness-blocking influence on your life:

1. *Dispute your personalized conclusions*. Others' values, positions, and outlooks as they are directed toward you are not you. In not passing judgment on yourself in relationship to others' judgments about you, you avoid putting yourself at the mercy of and trapping yourself by another's opinions and tastes. Avoid all appearances of self-evaluation by mastering self-acceptance coping ideas such as:

- "Others' opinions don't equal me."
- "Approval is nice but not necessary."
- "I can stand and possibly even develop a high level of immunity to criticism."
- "I accept the challenge of not passing judgment on myself."
- "Often people won't pleasantly treat me in direct proportion to how nicely I treat them - tough beans!"
- "I'd best accept that fairness never has and probably never will exist."
- "I don't have to be the one person in the universe who always gets a fair return on emotional investment."
- "Others have a right to their opinion - but it does not represent me."
- "What I think of myself is much more important than what someone else thinks of me."
- "To be criticized is disappointing but not a disaster; sad but not tragic; a hassle but not a horror."

2. *Stay with the hurt.* Tolerate the discomfort rather than hastily transforming it to anger. This allows you to set some boundaries on your turmoil by concentrating on limiting your exposure to the original upset. Then, strongly challenge your irrational belief system that caused and cultivates the hurt, as illustrated in the Part I diagram (pp. 12-13).
3. *Boldly admit to self-pity.* Humans seem especially hesitant to own the facts of feeling sorry for themselves. Yet, until one honestly identifies with this self-pampering trait, unshackling oneself from its unsettling effects will be left undone.
4. *Understand the other's motivation.* Other's intentions likely reflect that they are for themselves and their ideas rather than against you. Such a clearheaded view takes some of the strain out of disappointment and distances hurtful tendencies.
5. *See that dehumanization is self-inflicted.* Feelings of inferiority in relation to another's bias of you can only be brought on if you pass judgment on yourself because of another's disregard for things about you. Avoid the self-report card and you will avoid feeling humiliated.

6. *Look at the part of the relationship that is full.* Try not to judge the complete association by one contrary part of it. If you defocus on the other's unkind conduct while appreciating more favorable parts of the relationship, you won't take a lack of favoritism toward you so seriously.
7. *Remind yourself that people defend their values* (and that their defensiveness doesn't equal you). Oftentimes, people defend their ideas and ideals harshly. They have a difficult time not following their own nose when it comes to what they insist is right. Call to mind that this natural process has nothing to do with your value to yourself as a human; and you'll be able to cut yourself some further emotional slack.
8. *Get at fictional dependencies.* As you convince yourself that another's favorable review is nice but not necessary you lessen the trappings of dependency. In doing so you undo the basis for hurt. Extracting requirements for approval pulls out the self-blame option. When you don't need something there is nothing to blame yourself for when you don't have it.
9. *No self-downing for slips.* Because you are human to some degree you are by nature oversensitive. Work hard against your prickly nature! However, do so in an anti-perfectionistic way that allows you a margin for error. When you do err and foolishly make yourself too thin-skinned, remind yourself of your intention to do so less often.
10. *Attribute to the other and contribute to yourself.* Alert yourself that others' conduct represents only their viewpoint and current state of mind and not a reflection on you. In doing so you will contribute to your emotional well-being by affording the luxury of being yourself without painstakingly trying to prove yourself.
11. *See yourself as a majority of one.* Follow Thoreau's idea that "any man more right than his neighbor constitutes a majority of one" - that "public opinion is a weak tyrant compared with our own private opinion." Learn to trust yourself and your ability to rise above others' opinions by fully appreciating your potential for emotional self-reliance. Then, act on your self-sufficiencies in taking a

more free-wheeling stance on the outcome. Act more on your own behalf, yet personalize less.

Increase your visibility of this slippery, sometimes disguised, imposing but often impostor of an emotion called hurt. Then, try out the advice in this guide and see if you don't decrease emotional liability and increase your alive-ability and live-ability skill assets. Discover the advantages of living without the burden of this mysterious feeling state hanging over your head, and realize your capacity to do so.

PART I - THE ANATOMY OF HURT

A →	B →	C →	D →	E
(Activating event, something happens or is experienced)	(Belief system, what you tell yourself about his negative comments)	(Emotional consequences, your feelings - this is the initial, briefer, less observable problem)	(Forcefully debate, dispute, put forth a different way of thinking about his ill-considerate manner)	(New effects, feel differently)
For example, close associate harshly and unfairly criticizes you even though you have been exceptionally kind and considerate to him.	B_1 "What's wrong with me that I can't get someone important to treat me favorably?"	Hurt Betrayal Sulkiness	D_1 "Where is the evidence that because my associate treats me badly that there is something wrong with me? Do not humans often select against one another and does not their bias mainly tell what is important to them and their mood at the time?"	Disappointment Regret Do, take action rather than stew
	B_2 "How unfair that such unfairness and injustices be directed my way - poor me."		D_2 "Who says that justice must always triumph in my life? Where is it written that when fairness does not prevail that I have to whine, moan, squawk, gnash my teeth, or otherwise sulk about it?"	

B_3 This person's uncalled-for antics are horrible - I can't stand getting the short end of the relationship stick - it's too much to bear."	D_3 "Is there really any proof that I cannot survive, co-exist with, and highly tolerate another's unfair, annoying antics? I'd best cut myself some slack on the drama and lighten up a bit."
B_4 "What a louse I am for not getting more respect from this person and what a louse I am for not coping with the discrimination more strongly - I'm weak - I stink!"	D_4 "How can it be verified that because somebody treats me badly that I'm then bad? Why am I required to be a pillar of mental health when faced with discrimination? I'll try to cope well with it and then go on to something else."

PART II - EMOTIONAL SUBSTITUTION OF ANGER FOR HURT

A →	B →	C →	D →	E
(Activating event, something happens or is experienced)	(Belief system, what you tell yourself about feeling hurt)	(Emotional consequences, your feelings - this is the more dramatic, life-producing feeling that you kick into gear to erase the weak, empty feeling in your gut)	(Forcefully debate, dispute, put forth a different way of thinking about the fact you feel hurt)	(New effects, feel differently)
Feelings of hurt	B_1 "He's making me feel bad and has no right to do so - it's all his fault I'm feeling out of sorts and he's to blame."	Anger Rage	D_1 "Has it ever been proven that magic exists? How can someone transplant feelings into my gut without permission? I'm responsible for creating my own emotions - I make myself feel hurt by my personalized beliefs, and anything I believe I can disbelieve."	Annoyance Irritation Protect self from the other rather than condemn the other

B_2 "How awful that he would purposefully say those dastardly things that devastate me - I can't stand to be put down like this."	D_2 "How will another's criticisms hurt me in anyway? For one thing, nobody can put me down but me. I can tolerate another's bias without beating myself over the head with it."
B_3 "He deserves to be condemned for hurting me - that bastard - he stinks."	D_3 "Can it be proven that if someone acts badly that he is bad? Granted, such spiteful conduct is probably a signal that my associate is feeling badly, and how unfortunate that he is attempting to take his misery out on me - I'd best do well in protecting myself from him, without condemning him."

The Green-Eyed Monster Is Yellow: Jealousy as Fear and Insecurity

Jealousy is misplaced fear: What appears as mistrust of someone else actually reflects being ill at ease with oneself. Having less confidence in your partner's faithfulness often mirrors a diminished confidence in yourself. Likewise, trusting your partner to be alone indicates your capacity to stand alone. Accepting yourself provides the assurance necessary to accept time apart as natural and helpful to your relationship.

People who act in a jealous manner find it difficult to stand on their own two feet. They demand a safety valve to back up their insecurity. They fear for their emotional existence and then insist that they can't get along without a guaranteed return attachment. They insist the relationship be on their own terms rather than on "our" terms. They use anger in a desperate attempt to control for certainty in a world of relationships where there is none. They worry about being left out in the cold and frantically use intimidation to disguise their emotional weakness.

With their overreactions and self-doubts, they not only make themselves miserable but also defeat the relationship they wish to accommodate. Then they "pass the buck" emotionally by pinning the responsibility for their upset on their partner. Their solution to the problem is this: "Because you're to blame for my problems and disturbances, you must only conduct yourself in ways that I approve of so that I can then feel better. If you continue to conduct yourself in ways that meet with my displeasure, I will have no other choice but to continue to hound, hawk, and harass you until you become reasonable and do things my way (or until I drive you away, whichever comes first)!"

Fortunately, there are alternatives to this saga of fear and insecurity. Jealousy is often a right emotion that is put on the wrong horse. Because of this, misunderstandings regarding responsibility for and correction of this feeling state abound.

As Albert Ellis points out in his book, *The Civilized Couple's Guide to Extramarital Adventure*, there is a distinction between rational jealousy (emotional concern) and irrational jealousy (emotional consumption). The first contributes to human incentive. Because a fairly certain way to fail is to be petrified by the possibility of failure, the second detracts from activities that create happiness.

Like all emotional disturbance, jealousy begins with a wish, want, or desire that gets blocked, rerouted, or derailed. When the original preference is multiplied into a demand, emotional disturbance erupts. For instance, a healthy concern - or rational jealousy - could be expressed like this: "I want my partner to value fidelity as much as I do and as much as she says she does, and if it was discovered that this was not the case I would feel keenly saddened by such a disappointing turn of events."

On the other hand, unhealthy emotional desperation - irrational jealousy - will be promoted by strongly stating to yourself "Because I want my mate to value relationship faithfulness with as much passion as I do, he must (should, has to, has got to, ought to) do so, because I couldn't tolerate such a value conflict."

Stick with the *preference* and you will create emotional concern; extend the want to a *demand* or command (in the form of the *must*) and you will bring on emotional consumption. The chart on pages 26 and 27 further explores the anatomy of jealousy by illustrating which ways of thinking promote which emotions.

Calling to mind those ideas and background philosophies that contribute to better emotional and relationship equilibrium will allow for more endearing relationships that jealousy would otherwise contaminate. Jealous-acting people are fearful people who in their attempts to control, intimidate, and manipulate push away those they are trying desperately to pull toward them. The following additional guidelines can be part of a road map leading toward a destination of emotional security, which will result in more secure relationships.

1. *Identify and challenge the specific ideas you wish to surrender.* From the chart on pages 26 and 27 and from your own observations, highlight those ideas that create unwanted jealousy and then challenge them using the following method (reminding yourself that anything you believe you can disbelieve):

   - *Irrational idea that you wish to surrender:* "My partner should only act in ways that I find comforting; if he really loves me he always will."
     Dispute (ask yourself): "Where is the evidence that supports this belief and why?"
     Answer: "There is no such evidence. There are many reasons for this including the fact that my partner has free will, not my will, and can therefore choose his own values, even if they directly conflict with mine."
     List countering rational ideas:
     a. "My partner doesn't owe me anything, including his cherished faithfulness."
     b. "I don't always have to feel comfortable, and I am responsible for any discomfort that I create, *not* my partner."
     c. "Because my partner may act in a displeasing manner may have nothing to do with love or the price of spinach!"
     d. "My partner is acting in a contrary way - too damned bad! The sun isn't going to burn out nor is the moon likely to turn to green cheese because of it!"

- *Irrational idea that you wish to surrender:* "I have to police my partner's every activity, because if I don't, she might go astray and then I would have nothing."
  Dispute (ask yourself): "Where is the evidence that supports this idea and why?"
  Answer: "There is no evidence in that (a) I really don't have to do anything and I could choose not to hassle her, and (b) even if I did lose her I would still have myself - the same person I had before I met her."
  List countering rational ideas:
  a. "Dogging her may contribute to bringing on what I wish to avoid."
  b. "I contribute to this relationship too - therefore we *both* stand to lose something."
  c. "I don't have to examine what could happen with a fine-tooth comb; to think that I do only puts more pressure on both of us."

- *Irrational idea that you wish to surrender:* "If my partner betrayed our exclusive contract that would turn me into a bigger do-do than I already am."
  Dispute (ask yourself): "Where is the evidence that supports this idea and why?"
  Answer: "If my partner betrayed me this would be a distinct disadvantage in that I would lose an ideal I think a lot of. However, (a) I wouldn't have to judge myself by this or any other disadvantage that I have, (b) nor would I have to evaluate myself by someone else's behavior that goes against my wishes. There is evidence that if others honor our valued requests we are often better off and if they don't go along with our wishes we are frequently worse off. However, there is no proof that if someone does or doesn't comply with our desires we are a better or worse person. Rather, we are the same person regardless of the outcome of someone else's favors toward or selection against us."
  List countering rational ideas:
  a. "Others' fickle behavior does not equal me."

b. "I don't require another's loyalty to accept myself."
c. "I don't have to judge myself about anything and I'd best not try, because humans are unratable to begin with."
d. "Second fiddle doesn't mean second class."
e. "Self-acceptance doesn't require external props - it is something I can always do for myself - by myself."
f. "Nothing can demean me but me - and I've got better things to do with my time and energy."

- *Irrational idea that you wish to surrender:* "I couldn't bear it if my partner turned away from me because facing life alone would be intolerable."
  Dispute (ask yourself): "Where is the evidence that supports this idea and why?"
  Answer: "There is no evidence that I couldn't hold up emotionally if my partner exited our relationship because (a) I got along by myself before I met him so that proves my capability of riding the tide alone, and (b) as long as I remain a living, breathing human being one of the things I can always do is tolerate something."
  List countering rational ideas:
  a. "Being alone does not have to be lonely."
  b. "Being left high and dry and forced to depend more upon myself could prove to be of benefit to me in its own way."
  c. "I could stand what I wouldn't like."
  d. "That wouldn't be fair - which would be all the more reason to be fair to myself."
  e. "If love is no longer being served at the table, move on to a different setting."
  f. "I wouldn't have to take a bad situation and make it worse."
  g. "I wouldn't be required to devastate myself about difficulties."
  h. "That would be a sad part of my life - but not bigger than my life."

2. *Purposeful production of counter behaviors.* The most direct way to change an irrational idea is to take action against it. Solicit the help of your partner by directly explaining your intention to work against your problem of jealousy. Then, request that your partner purposefully act in ways that you have previously upset yourself about, such as talking to attractive members of the opposite sex when you are out together; calling members of the opposite sex for general conversation (perhaps former boyfriends/girlfriends or mates); being friendly with other male/female friends at work (and after work); and not being available every time you call and intentionally not explaining his or her whereabouts. Such contradictory requests expose your problem to a real life laboratory in which you can create an immunity to it.
3. *Daily doses of rational-emotive imagery.* This imagery exercise allows you to practice working on your problems without being in an actual circumstance. Follow these steps:

   - Close your eyes and vividly picture yourself in the situation that you typically make yourself jealous in, for example, when your partner makes it obvious that he or she is enjoying social conversation with a member of the opposite sex.
   - Force yourself to feel in your typical jealous manner.
   - Substitute the different emotion of concern for jealousy by pushing yourself to think differently about this old problem. Call to mind some of the previous coping ideas and create some of your own in order to do this.
   - Bask in the advantages of your efforts to lighten up, regardless of how ever so slightly you have been able to give yourself some emotional slack. Practice this procedure twice a day, 5 to 10 minutes each time, until your more deliberate perspective becomes more second nature. Then, in the future when you are in a situation of concern you will be more likely to call on your method of clearer thinking.

4. *Cultivate a philosophy of permissiveness.* See that not only do others have a right to betray your values and are not to be condemned for doing so, but you also are not mandated to always do the right thing and need not damn yourself when you don't. Have compassion for yourself in the aftermath of your jealousy. Pledge yourself to consistently work against this handicapping emotion, but don't put yourself down when you wrongly create it. As you take pressure off yourself for having this problem you will likely be better able to work against it.
5. *Get rid of fixed ideas.* Discard thoughts that presume necessity. For ideas such as *"my partner should, must, has to, ought to, has got to, is required to* act only in ways that I deem acceptable," substitute ideas that address the reality that "although it would be nice if my partner acted in ways of my choosing it is not necessary that her conduct only mirror what I define as acceptable behavior."
6. *Don't put all your eggs in one basket.* The more you learn how to entertain yourself and the more diversity in life you self-discover via taking on more *nonloving* interests, the less jealous you are likely to make yourself when your partner acts in self-determined ways.
7. *Be glad you're concerned.* Valuing your relationship enough to oversee it in a concerned way will generate the healthy interest to kindle the spark in it. Fearfully scrutinizing it with a fine-tooth comb will likely light the unhealthy kind of fire that will burn it out. Taking it for granted can be avoided by closely observing ongoing relationship festivities without obsession. Such alert monitoring can be welcomed as a form of upkeep of gaining and maintaining togetherness.
8. *Show a comprehensive interest in your partner.* Give your partner the message that you're not only interested in him or her for what he or she can do for you, but also for what he or she can do for himself or herself. Do this by encouraging him or her to do things he or she enjoys away from you. This will have the dual advantage of making yourself harder to resist while acting against controlling, dependent tendencies.
9. *Avoid a master-slave mentality.* Understand that you don't "let" your partner do certain things and act in de-

termined ways. Your mate has a mind of his or her own and independently chooses his or her conduct. Your only choice is whether you are going to complain and hassle your mate about his or her actions.

10. *Adopt a philosophy of flexible closeness.* A mother and her teenage daughter were walking along the beach. The daughter inquired as to how the mother and the daughter's father had remained married for so many years. The mother said nary a word. Instead, she picked up a handful of sand and began squeezing it. The harder she squeezed, the more sand she lost. Finally, she let up on her grip and as she did, the sand remained solidly in her hand. Rotation and balance between time together and time apart are the best by-words when trying to retain refreshened relationship capacities.
11. *Expect no blank check.* Avoid the one-sided view that your partner has nothing better to do than to accommodate your every value. This childlike assumption runs counter to the mature reality of free will - your partner's freedom to establish his or her will and not your will in every way and everyday decisions.
12. *Overcome fears of being alone.* Worrying about your mate abandoning you and the presumed absolute horror of being alone makes for a desperate approach to heading off this supposed calamity. Instead, envision yourself standing alone and experiencing the rights and advantages thereof. Putting a dent in your fear habit will likely free up compatibility potential that you otherwise would have suffocated.
13. *Illuminate advantages.* Highlight what life would be like if you curtailed your jealousy problem. Such a listing could include not only the advantages a less pressured relationship would bring, but also general gains that you would experience from using your problems of relationship fusion and overattachment to become a more tolerant, self- and other-accepting person generally.
14. *Practice transparency and antishamefulness.* Openly admit your insecure tendencies toward making yourself into a little child in adult's clothing - along with your intentions to reverse such inclinations. Such revelations remove the pressures of secrecy, minimize second-level

problems of shame about having the flaw, and pave the way for reducing your undue feelings of threat.

15. *Practice bilevel self-acceptance principles:*

    - Learn to accept yourself apart from any relationship advantages you desire. As you learn to better trust yourself to sustain yourself emotionally, you remove the fearful roots of your insecurity. Not relying on another's acceptance of you to accept yourself frees you up emotionally to sensibly invest in the practical upkeep of the relationship.
    - When you slip yourself into a temporary jealous state, don't turn it into a major setback. Avoid the double whammy of mistakenly pushing yourself off the wagon and condemning yourself besides. Instead, acknowledge your blunder in the present and inspire yourself to make fewer of them in the future.

16. *Take on a philosophy of challenge*. Jealousy is a tough problem. Tough-minded and forced-acting solutions are therefore in order. Strengthen your resolve to push yourself beyond present boundaries of fear and insecurity. Such ideas of sustained effort are likely to assist in sustaining relationships you value.

Beyond the previously described options, what choices do you have? The more you squeeze, the more life and love in your relationship you will likely lose. The more you try to push your partner in the direction you think is right, the more likely he or she will be to pull toward the position he or she thinks is correct. Likewise, the more you take a step back rather than two steps forward, care less without becoming uncaring, the more you will likely be able to enjoy the fruits of the person you care about. To avoid this pendulum that will sway you toward relationship seasickness, color your feelings neither green nor yellow, but with a hue that is artistically and scientifically in your and your loved ones best interest for survival and happiness.

Thoughts That Create Healthy Concern About A Relationship (Rational Jealousy)	Rational Background Philosophy	Thoughts That Create Unwanted Desperation (Irrational Jealousy)	Irrational Background Philosophy
"I hope my partner keeps his end of the bargain because I value the exclusiveness that we have agreed upon."	People are capable of getting along without certain significant other people.	"My partner has to always keep our original agreement and has no right to change his mind."	I can't accept myself so others couldn't either.
"I wish my partner wouldn't put herself in situations that I view as risk factors for our previously discussed fidelity and I intend to discuss this very concern with her."	Because something could happen does not mean it is going to happen - but if it does it can be coped with.	"My partner should only go places and only conduct herself in ways that I am comfortable with - and if she really loves me that is what she will always do."	Because I have very little to offer this relationship except unquestioned fidelity, my partner is required to continually answer to me about her plans to stay true to me and only me.
"It would be sad and disappointing if my mate decided to give in to everyday temptations in that this would directly violate a primary condition of our relationship and perhaps bring an end to something I cherish."	Being forced to expand oneself by relying more on oneself can further self-development.	"If my partner betrays our agreement I couldn't make it through the night alone - I don't trust myself to be able to handle life if I were to lose him."	If one doesn't worry about the possibility of bad things happening - bad things will happen.
	Disappointments are not disasters.		
	Both partners make contributions to successful relationships and therefore each has good reasons to think	"I have to brood about, stew over, and hound my partner	There are guarantees in life and love and I have to find such assured security to be able to function. My partner is re-

"Because we *both* stand to lose a lot if our faithfulness agreements are violated I think that it would be best to address my concerns."

"Because it is possible that my mate could decide to be unfaithful to me does not mean I have to keep dwelling on and brooding about this event happening."

"Being forced to get along by myself might not be easy but I could bear it."

"I can tolerate the uncertainty of not knowing 100% that my partner is 100% true blue."

twice before violating the terms of the relationship contract.

To monitor and update a relationship you value is good - to scrutinize it is bad.

Participants in relationships have free will and to assume otherwise would be undemocratic.

about the possibility of her leaving, because if I don't, she will leave - and that would be unbearable."

"I have to cling to what I have because if I don't hang on for dear life I might lose him - and then I, who am nothing to begin with, would have nothing."

sponsible for my insecurities and owes it to me to take care of them and me by appeasing and pacifying me by becoming a clone of what I expect from him.

Anger as Addiction And Nerve Gas

Of all the human emotions, anger is probably misrepresented the most. Not only does it disguise hurt, fear, and emotional dependency and have components of demandingness, condemnation, and punitiveness, but it also has often-overlooked rudiments of addiction and artificial courage.

Anger is often produced as the emotion of choice over the hurt that precedes it, because one can more powerfully hang one's emotional hat on spite and outrage than on the self-belittlement that accompanies hurt. Hurtful feelings of self-depreciation can quickly be converted into a supposed stronghold of anger by the simple statement: "You hurt me - you bastard!" Making oneself emotionally dependent on others' alleged lifeline accommodations invites fear that reflects (a) an urgency about losing what has been defined as mandatory, and (b) a wrong assumption about what others can do to you - as shown by the thinking that others can dislike things about you and diminish you by their dislike. Anger is pressed into desperate action as an attempt to intimidate, manipulate, and control for what are thought to be essential advantages. This guide will expose and focus on the common, yet often neglected, addictive and assertive ingredients of anger.

When something feels good there tends to be a nostalgia for it, a longing to return to it, even if it's not good for you.

The human tendency is to shortsightedly reattach oneself to "feel good" experiences even if in the long haul they will handicap you. The more you practice something like anger expression, the more convenient it is to tempt yourself to continue along the same lines, even when that activity opposes long-range survival objectives.

When in the throes of gratifying and indulging oneself in expression of anger, feelings of absolute superiority frequently abound. When feeling spite you can think whatever you want about other people, and they can't do a thing about it. Recalling such heightened feelings of control makes it convenient to manufacture anger. This reflects your addicting yourself to the energizing, adrenalin-flowing components of this otherwise self-defeating emotion. Practicing the bad habit of expressing anger allows you to temporarily feel good while blowing off steam but, like other addictions, it will likely result in long-range complications that will contaminate your goals for health and happiness.

As a motivator, anger also pays a price. Anger can be a red-eyed incentive that will help stimulate you to stand up for yourself. It will also result in your walking all over your social group. Such outrage is not necessary either to protect yourself or to go after what you want. You don't need to be angry to get out of the way of an oncoming train. In fact, if you do make yourself upset in such a circumstance, you are likely to stumble and increase the risk of injury. This is one of the main hazards of anger as incentive; it presses you into action, but once in motion it increases the risk of negative effects and decreases the possibility of reaching your goals.

Anger as nerve gas enables you to do things you would be too timid to do under the influence of everyday moods. However, because tunnel vision and revenge motives accompany anger, you are likely to do things that in the long run will work against you. Acting out of control as a means of gaining control is contradictory; you cannot accomplish two opposing behaviors at the same time. Such double-think notions will cause you to "cook your own goose." Anger represents the illusion of gaining control - when actually you're losing control. You also lose the advantages you might gain from a more well-rounded motivational stance.

Striving for what you want in order to gain practical advantages, being able to express your wishes purposefully, and choosing to stand up on your own behalf allow you to accomplish your goals while minimizing emotional flack. Having dissatisfactions in life and expressing your grievances, or attempting to work around obstacles to what you believe to be the good life *without* blowing up these concerns into emotional disturbance are more efficient means of extending the effort required to reach your goals. Clearheaded, step-by-step efforts will result from telling yourself statements such as "I want, wish, would like, prefer certain people and/or special circumstances in my life to be different, and I'm going to do what I can to influence them constructively."

On the other hand, statements such as the following will amplify what you find highly desirable into essential, mandatory conditions: "Because I want, wish, would like, prefer certain people and/or specific circumstances in my life to be different, therefore they have to, must, should, ought to be the way I find them preferable." This type of statement will inject components of disturbance and self-defeat into your problem-solving agenda. Staying away from self-anointed attempts to rearrange the universe and people in it allows you to go after the goals that are right for you, for the right reasons, in a more open-minded, deliberate - but determined - manner.

Like other emotional disturbances, anger is caused by distorted thinking. It might be helpful to break down the belief systems that will move you away from the addictive, nerve gas components - irrational anger - toward more controlled, helpful feelings of rational annoyance and irritation.

Anger is irrational because it is essentially against your best interests, whereas annoyance or irritation are considered rational in that these feeling states are in your best interests. With anger the goals are made out to be to hurt other people, teach them a lesson that they won't soon forget, and show them what a holier-than-thou person you are and what unworthier-than-all people they are. Making yourself feel healthy annoyance or irritation instead of anger will grant the lateral views required to not let others take advantage of you; thus conditions that can be changed are changed constructively, and you'll be better able to accept any remaining frustrations.

The statements on page 35 illustrate the process of detecting beliefs and discriminating those that invite constructive emotions and behaviors from those that bring on destructive feelings and actions.

When you realize that you have created anger as part of your life and you wish to brainstorm better ways to spend your time, consider the following practical suggestions:

1. Because chance favors the prepared mind, and because repetition is the mother of learning, drill yourself with the countering, contrasting ways of thinking listed previously. Being able to recall these coping ideas as well as you can your telephone number or middle initial will help you to nip anger-producing beliefs in the bud. Anger can be dissolved without expression by changing your irrational beliefs that produce it.
2. Understand that there is more than one way to motivate yourself. Anger need not accompany the perseverance, persistence, and dogged determination required to achieve your goals or stand up for yourself.
3. Focus on the long-range disadvantages rather than the short-range indulgences of this harmful emotion.
4. See that blowing off steam doesn't change the dependent, demanding, intolerant views that insist that the world and everyone in it be just like you.
5. Correct the faulty notion of "the more you express anger, the less angry you become." See instead that the more you practice overreacting the better overreactor and the bigger emotional baby you become. One of the common misconceptions about anger is that if you "get in touch" with your angry feelings and express them, they will somehow magically go away.
6. See that anger frequently boomerangs. Reinforcing anger with practice is likely to result in it going out the back door but coming in the front.
7. Remind yourself that although expressing anger may feel wallowingly good, it is not good for you.
8. Pick up on the idea that releasing your tendencies to get hot under the collar is *not* a show of strength. Rather, it openly puts your traits of insecurity and immaturity on display with your overdone responses.

9. Work on developing confidence in being restrained while seeing that what is written about the alleged harmful effects of controlling rather than expressing anger is much overplayed. See instead that much more harm has been done through anger expression than anger restraint (e.g., literal destruction of relationships, families, nations, civilizations).
10. Don't view anger (or anything else) as self-proving. See that you're not beholding to anyone and that you would do better to be yourself with your social group without trying to prove yourself to your associates.
11. Recognize that at best anger is a very poor way to gain and maintain someone else's attention. Such a dramatic act waters down your message, because others are likely to respond to your anger and miss the content of your directive. Once the dust is settled the receiver of your wrath is likely to avoid you as if you had a contagious disease.
12. Introduce to yourself the notion of preventing anger from building up rather than letting it build up; then concentrate on response prevention. Once you allow anger to well up close to the surface, a quick-triggered response becomes riskier. Don't let your anger gain momentum. Put the brakes on it sooner rather than later or an escalating, multiplying effect will likely result.
13. See that you don't "let" others be themselves or grant them "permission" to choose their values. Rather, those matters of others' choices are their right, at their and not your discretion. Your only option is whether you're going to hassle them about exercising their prerogative. Reminding yourself that you are not ordained to run others' lives can be humbling.
14. Put a dent in the notion "it's easier to get angry" (probably because you have practiced this bad habit all your life). Instead, realize that as hard as it may be to restrain yourself, it's harder not to because of the emotional fallout and practical disadvantages suffered in the aftermath of such childish expression.
15. Realize that hate is a four-letter word and that when you spite someone who has wronged you, you become like that other person in that you take on the same condemning, childish notions that he or she has.

16. Take a very close look at your emotional dependency as a core factor in your fire-and-brimstone emotions. Realize that anger does *not* better establish you as a more independent, self-sufficient person. In contrast, understand that you will mainly make yourself angry at those that you make yourself dependent upon. So, build a huge case for emotional independence by seeing that others' favors are a nice but not necessary part of your life. The less dependent and the more self-accepting that you make yourself, the less angry you will become.

In the final analysis, see your anger for what it is - a futile, childish attempt to manipulate, control, and intimidate others. Such actions may, in their own distorted, disturbed way, feel better in an addictive way and motivate you to produce action at the same time in the short run. However, they are likely to result in your getting worse; they are likely to manufacture the type of harsh consequences that result in sabotaging constructive goals in the long run. Changing your views of what anger means for you may not produce the ideal world in which you achieve to your *fullest* extent of living *happily ever after* - though it may well result in your accomplishing to your *fuller* extent while living *happier*. Give peace a chance and learn for yourself!

Irrational Anger as Against Your Best Interests	Contrasting Ideas That Result in Feelings of Annoyance and Irritation as in Your Best Interests
• "Life has to change."	"Though I would like certain things in life to be different, there is no reason why anything in life has to be different than it is."
• "They should act differently."	"I wish they would act differently than they sometimes do, but there is no evidence anyone is required to cater to my wishes."
• "I need their cooperation and understanding and they hurt me when they don't provide me with these essential, mandatory requirements, those bastards."	"Although I would like and hope for their cooperation and understanding, it's far from mandatory that I get it, and I don't have to needlessly upset myself when I don't get it."
• "It's terrible and horrible when they act that way."	"Such antics are disappointing but not a calamity."
• "I can't stand it this way."	"I don't like it this way, but I can damn well stand what I don't like."
• "They have no right to be wrong; who do they think they are?"	"They have free will, not my will - after all, I don't run the universe yet (though I do admit that I sometimes feverously and foolishly try to)!"
• "Others *must not* do what I don't want and *must only* do what I want them to do."	"People aren't required to convenience my wishes and wants by giving me my piece of taffy - to demand otherwise is undemocratic and godlike."
• "They stink - I can't stand them."	"Condemn the sin but not the sinner. I can tolerate, put up with, stomach though not necessarily like others' contrary, dissatisfying actions."

Saying "No" - With or Without Feeling Guilty

You can protect your time, energy, and personal planning by setting boundaries on your willingness to refuse others' requests when it is in your best interest to do so. People often believe that this cannot be accomplished while feeling guilty. This guide suggests that although it is preferable to avoid guilt in choosing not to exhaust yourself for someone else's convenience, you can take your guilt with you in not doing so, and in the process act against the faulty ideas behind this handicapping emotion. The best way to change a false idea is to act against it. By consistently acting in self-interested ways, you challenge the following guilt-producing beliefs:

- "I shouldn't say 'no' to those I associate with."
- "I have to have others' approval and could not tolerate being disliked for my imposing deprivations on them."
- "I couldn't stand it if my associates feel hurt after I refuse them."
- "I have no right to betray another's wishes."
- "I don't have it in me to say 'no.' "
- "It's so awful that I feel nervous and queasy when I refuse someone's request that I can't stand it."
- "If I don't feel guilty when I say 'no,' this means that I am an uncaring person."

- "If I dissatisfy someone in my social group I might be gossiped about, rumored to be a hard-ass; and that would cause me to melt."
- "If I say 'no,' all hell might break loose, and I find conflicts unbearable."

Guilt has two basic components: (a) I did something bad, and therefore (b) I'm bad. Uproot these beliefs by understanding that not overextending yourself in the service of others is actually a plus if you value personal well-being. Also, the fact that you are not willing to sacrifice yourself to accommodate others doesn't turn you into an evil being.

Take guilt as a special form of anxiety with you and transform it in both thought and deed. Give yourself the practical advantages that limit setting can bring. Frequent practice of your assertive activity along with repeatedly reminding yourself of the following rational self-comments is likely to create more of an immunity to any accompanying discomfort.

- "Because I could say 'yes' to another's request doesn't mean I should (or have to)."
- "True, if I deprive someone, he may well disapprove of if not dislike me. That would be highly regretful, but hardly disastrous."
- "If my relationship with my associate is based on never-ending cooperation, perhaps it's not a very solid association to begin with."
- "The world is full of people who often select against someone else's wishes, so obviously there is no universal law against this right."
- "I am not dependent on others' approval; when I make myself so I set myself up to feel fear of and anger toward them."
- "I am not responsible for another's upsets; it is doubtful whether I can transplant hurt or any other emotion to someone else."
- "Because I have had some difficulty saying 'no' on my behalf up until now, it does not mean that I cannot start a new pattern."
- "I'm not in the world to feel comfortable 24 hours a day, and I'd better stop complaining about discomforts that come with the territory called change."

- "Not feeling guilty when I say 'no' is actually a very caring act; it proves that I care enough about myself to not make myself feel miserable about a decision I made - which, come to think of it, is likely to make me a more fun, caring person to be around."
- "Conflict is not pleasurable, but it takes two to fight. I can choose to take a step back rather than two steps forward in approaching it while caring less without becoming uncaring."

Advantages to putting your best foot forward on your own behalf - with or without feeling guilty - include the following:

1. *Makes you harder to resist.* As a result of freeing yourself up emotionally you are likely to be enjoyed more by others. Less dependent, minimally anxious, and less angry-acting people are usually more often favored by their social group.
2. *Increases personal happiness.* Having more time for activities you enjoy and special interests that absorb you accommodates the pursuit of happiness.
3. *Encourages others' self-sufficiency.* Knowing that they cannot routinely depend on you makes it convenient for your associates to increase their potential for self-reliance and skill development.
4. *Encourages a more well-rounded relationship.* By demonstrating that love, friendship, colleague relationships, and obligations don't go hand in glove, you contribute to the depth of the association. Practicing the idea that the relationship can stand the test of controversy while extending its dimensions may result in a fuller appreciation of it.
5. *Injects a vote of confidence.* The message behind a straightforward refusal to comply is, "I think you can handle the disappointment, so I'm not going to treat you like an emotional cripple by tiptoeing around and making excuses for my refusal." Such positive expectations encourage another's tolerance and acceptance levels.
6. *Promotes relationship informality, honesty, and freewheelingness.* Relationships can be more fully enjoyed against a background of openness. Knowing where you

stand with someone takes away the guesswork involved in relationship upkeep and can provide a loosening and lightening up effect.

7. *Affords the opportunity to practice being yourself without trying to prove yourself.* Getting yourself past sacred requirements of others' acceptance and approval (which precedes compulsive agreement and compliance) establishes a more solid self-acceptance baseline. Self-proving activity is perhaps the main avenue by which humans give themselves problems. Actions that document self-reliance in spite of others' potential dislike provide a foundation to overcome this self-proving tendency.
8. *Leads to gains within gains.* By actively countering the approval principle (i.e., "I need the approval of all significant others in my life, and I couldn't tolerate risking losing such seals of approval"), you begin to establish a different philosophy about your presumed requirements from others. This ability can then be used in future circumstances where you tend to bind yourself up with emotional dependency.

Why wait? Doing what is in your long-range best interest has value - with or without making yourself feel guilty. As you challenge your self-downing, guilt-producing ideas, take action on behalf of yourself and gain the practical advantages thereof. You can't turn your guilt off and on like a light switch, but this does not mean that you can't dim its strength while giving these feelings time to catch up to your new non-blaming ideas. In the meantime, a self-directed stance will likely be of profit and encouragement not only to yourself, but also to those for whom you provide opportunities to learn how to better tolerate disappointment and a better appreciation of the value of not expecting others to do for them what they can just as well do for themselves.

He Who Hesitates Is Lost: Understanding and Overcoming Uncertainty, Indecision, and Confusion

In seeking a commitment to a plan of action from a client I asked, "Will you do it?" He promptly replied, "I'll give you a definite maybe." This double-think response left me not knowing any more about his choice than before I asked the question. His decision-making fence riding indicated that not only did he not know the answer to my question, but also that he was confusing himself about the process of making a clearheaded choice.

Humans often put themselves in the position of the fabled donkey who stood an equal distance between two haystacks but ended up starving to death because he was unable to decide which haystack to eat from. This guide will outline the following points about unsureness, including (a) definitions of uncertainty, indecision, and confusion; (b) descriptions of the common denominators of these difficulties as they reflect more general problems associated with the human condition, especially overreaction and self-evaluation; (c) some of the precise irrational ideas that block a more decisive approach to life; and (d) a review of specific suggestions that can get you past statements like "I used to be indecisive, but now I'm not sure."

DEFINITIONS

UNCERTAINTY

You can run, but you can't hide from uncertainty. It is a given part of the human territory. We live in an uncertain world. Uncertainty encourages the positive feeling of concern; without concern we would not be able to think very sharply when sorting out our options. Uncertainty only becomes a problem if you insist on finding a "sure thing" when there is no such thing. This is exactly what the indecisive-acting person does.

INDECISION

Indecision blooms by perfectionistically demanding tomorrow's answers today. This is the insistence that before the choice to go down path A is made, one must have knowledge that path B won't turn out better. Such demands are like trying to find a corner in a silo; they are likely to leave you spinning around and around indefinitely. This stubborn refusal to act in spite of uncertainty opens the floodgates of confusion.

CONFUSION

Feeling perplexed about choices is like applesauce - they all seem to run together. This out-of-sorts state of mind results from a combination of factors. Asking impossible questions about what may happen tomorrow, looking to others for direction and getting mixed advice, and wanting two things at the same time (e.g., to make the right choice minus any discomfort, or to take the right turn and have the approval of all those affected by your decision) will all cause your head to swim in the sea of self-inflicted confusion.

COMMON DENOMINATORS OF INDECISIVENESS

1. *Low frustration tolerance.* Exaggerating the consequences of a negative outcome of your decision will put you at your wit's end rather than help you choose. Hesi-

tation is promoted by convincing yourself that negative fallout from your decision would be more than you could tolerate (e.g., "I couldn't stand it if I made a choice and it turned out to be the wrong one").

2. *Self-judgments.* Believing that you would be a failure if you failed to make the right choice will stop you in your decision-making tracks faster than you can say "freeze." When you evaluate yourself by the outcome of your initiative, you leave yourself with too much to lose; this prompts you to cut back from that initiative. If you believe "I am my decisions, and if I make a bad choice, then I'm bad," you will find it convenient to avoid making a decision indefinitely.
3. *Magical thinking.* Believing that somebody, sometime, somewhere, somehow will take care of the matter under consideration without your taking a stand one way or another will stall your decision-making capacity. This fairy-tale notion assumes that if the dirt is swept under the rug, it will go away by itself. This is a far cry from the more realistic notion, "Doing gets it done."
4. *Perfectionism.* Waiting for the perfect moment, where time will stand still so you can then make the perfect choice, will keep you boxed in, rather than allowing you to bust out to make a choice - whether perfect or imperfect.
5. *Demands for certainty.* Childish insistence that the universe review for you all possible outcomes, along with assurances that the results from your decision will turn out favorably, will stop you in your decision-making tracks, pronto.
6. *Dire needs for acceptance and approval.* Making your decisions subject to the approval of all the people all of the time produces disapproval anxiety that disables your ability to decide in your best interest.
7. *Conflict anxiety.* Blowing out of proportion the discomfort from making decisions that run counter to others' wants encourages avoidance of choice.
8. *Guilt.* Believing yourself to be responsible for others who may have problems due to your decision further restricts your options in making the decision.

9. *Shame.* Fear of what public disclosure of your decisions will bring further limits choice possibilities.
10. *Other pity.* Feeling sorry for others who may be inconvenienced as a result of your decision walls off the possibility of making it.
11. *Self-pity.* Feeling sorry for yourself about your own disadvantage that may result from a difficult choice will prevent your paying the price that goes along with that decision.
12. *Overdecisiveness.* Just as indecisiveness often reflects a fear of failing to make the right choice, overdecisiveness often mirrors a fear of others' disapproval if you were to appear to have any hesitation. A fickle decision-making style - going from one extreme to the other - is used to frantically perfume these fears.
13. *Blaming others.* Inviting others to play the designated decision-making role allows you to blame them if their suggestions backfire. Waiting to solicit others' recommendations is a slick way to pass the responsibility for the decision's effect on you to someone else.

DECISION-MAKING BLOCKING IDEAS

People often come to their options with precise, faulty self-sentences that hinder the formation of a more elastic, well-rounded outlook on decision making. Some examples include:

- "Nothing bad can happen as long as I don't decide, so if I wait indefinitely nothing bad will ever happen."
- "If I make a decision I might fail to make the right one, and if I fail I'd be a schmuck, so I'll avoid failure and schmuckhood by not deciding."
- "Making bad choices and coping with the disadvantages this would bring would be too much to bear, the pits, impossible to live with. Rather than die such an excruciating death I'll avoid giving myself such an ordeal by deciding not to decide."
- "I have to know every angle of the effects of my decisions before I give myself the go-ahead to make them. To tread

toward unknown, uncertain territory that lies ahead is just too much to ask of myself."

- "If I make a decision, others might not approve of my choice. That would cause me to melt emotionally; rather than risk that happening I'll wait on rather than move toward a choice."
- "What happens if someone disagrees with my decision? I can't stand the discomfort of conflict, and if my views ran counter to someone else's, I don't know whether I could cope with these uneasy feelings."
- "I'm responsible for others' feelings and responses to my decisions. Others might feel badly about my choices so I'd better not make them. If this happened, I would be bad for making bad choices that others felt badly about."
- "To make such a clear-cut decision will put me in plain view of my social group. Such exposure would be embarrassing and humiliating if I flubbed my choices - so I'll avoid flubbing and discredit by holding to the center of the line."
- "Others in higher authority and with more experience than I should know what's best to do. Furthermore, they are required to share these exact answers with me. If they don't it's their fault if I make the wrong decision (and they are also to blame if they do tell me what to do and it turns out to be incorrect)."

SPECIFIC SUGGESTIONS

1. *Challenge your thinking.* Understand that it's not the possibility of making a wrong decision that is shattering but your shattering beliefs about such a happening. Thoughts that would help pave the way for more clear-cut and clearheaded decisions include:

    - "A sure way to fail is not to *make* a decision but to *not* make a decision; you don't avoid failure by not trying or deciding - you guarantee it."
    - "Decisions don't go away by sweeping them under a rug. I cannot not decide; to not choose is to decide to keep things as they are. Allowing decisions to accu-

mulate on the back burner will complicate my life further."

- "Weigh the options and make a decision; live with and learn from - even though you might not necessarily like - the results of your choice."
- "True, others may disapprove of my decision and pass judgment on me because of it. It's not true that I would be required to shame, stigmatize, humiliate, or harass myself because of it."
- "I am not responsible for others' overreactions to my decisions. I will consider the possible effects my choices have on others. However, I'd best have a sense of humility for what I can do to someone else and understand that others will affect themselves more by what they tell themselves about my decisions."
- "I don't have to intimidate myself about queasy, awkward feelings that I may give myself while making a decision that is in conflict with the grain of my social group."
- "Because others might know what they think is the better opinion does not require them to tell me; and if they do tell me they are not required to take the responsibility for the consequences that follow my choice to test out their suggestion."
- "I can afford to make decisions because I can afford the luxury of accepting myself when I make bad ones. True, if I make a decision I might fail to make the right one. It's untrue that I would be a failure because of it."

2. *See that there are no right or wrong decisions.* There are only decisions based on present evidence. Agreeing with yourself to decide based on the current information rather than insisting choices be made that are the "right" answers, allows you to go ahead and decide rather than wait for absolute certainty to appear.
3. *Imagine the relief.* Rather than focus on the discomfort you feel in making a choice, set your sights on the feelings of lighthearted delight in the aftermath of relieving yourself from the burden of suspended indecision.

4. *Fine-tune your calculations.* List the advantages and disadvantages of each of your options (e.g., to leave or remain in your current job). Assign points to each plus and each minus, with the total number of points not to exceed 100. Then see which fork of the road is estimated to have more advantages for you.
5. *Time yourself.* Set a time limit within which you contract with yourself to knock off the malarkey and move forward with your choice. Then. . . .
6. *Penalize yourself if you falter.* If you fail to stick with your self-imposed time limit, assign yourself a self-management penalty that would be more uncomfortable than the task of deciding (e.g., talk nicely to or send money to someone you don't like; get up 2 hours earlier each day in the next month; eat your least favorite meal each day for the next 2 weeks, etc.).
7. *Don't make the opposite mistake.* Guard against going from one extreme to the other to cover for your fence-riding ways. Making a hurried choice in order to lessen feelings of anxiety is the same self-defeating poison with a different label. Less thought doesn't mean little thought.
8. *Don't make self-judgments.* Asininely putting off making choices like the donkey described earlier doesn't make you an ass. Self-blame for having the trait of indecisiveness is likely to result in confusing yourself even more about your alternatives.
9. *Distinguish between pausing and hesitating.* Wanting to know as much as possible about your choices is different from insisting that you know everything about them. Wishing you knew tomorrow's answers today before you decide is a horse of a different color than demanding that you have to know before you get yourself off center. These wishes and wants will time limit your review of alternatives.
10. *See if prior knowledge is really all it's cracked up to be.* The reality of knowing life's happenings ahead of time is that life would be less lifelike. Being able to predict the future would likely bring boredom and listlessness. The alertness and energy from anticipation and participation would be lost in predictable outcomes.

11. *Realize that your state of mind is more important than the decision.* If you come to your decision with a clear-headed state of mind, your final choice is more likely to take care of itself. Getting yourself less upset about the possibility of making the wrong decision will increase your chances of making the right one.
12. *Use emotiveness.* Making a strong declaration to yourself about your choice helps make the connection between knowing what you want to do and convincing yourself of what you know. Making what you believe to be a good choice in a half-hearted way waters down the strength of your conviction.
13. *Promote a philosophy of challenge.* Overcoming human tendencies to overreact and personalize does not come easily. Understanding that making a wrong turn would not signal the end of the world nor diminish your value to yourself requires taking on tougher-minded and quicker-acting strategies. Taking on a philosophy of challenge in doing just that would likely bring advantages to many areas of your life.
14. *Examine but don't brood.* Reviewing the ins and outs of your range of choices will keep you well-informed. Dwelling on each detail gives you "paralysis of the analysis" regarding these options.
15. *Avoid double binds.* Boxing yourself in with exaggerated and self-blaming views whether you decided to do or not to do something is a no-win set-up. If you view betraying someone else's values by your decision as bigger than life and the worst of all possible crimes, or betraying your own values in deciding to please others as a similar calamity, you will end up damning yourself whether you do or don't.
16. *Distinguish uncertainty from insecurity.* Uncertainty is a given part of life in our uncertain world. Insecurity is the excess baggage that comes from taking your decisions and yourself too seriously. Fretting about and fearing failure are at its roots. Weighing alternatives in the face of uncertainty is good - getting yourself weighed down by them is not.

Decisions! Decisions! Ziggy said, "I used to be bothered by indecision, but now I just have a hard time making up my mind." In either case, time and progress in self-development are hindered by keeping the jury out beyond a reasonable time. Rather than creating a hung jury, make your own certainty-with-uncertainty verdict, and see if you don't free yourself from the bonds of indecision and confusion.

I Forgot to Remember to Forget: Guidelines for Relinquishing the Past

When clients go to great lengths to detail their personal history I often state, "That's B.C." The common question is then, "What's B.C.?" to which I reply, "before counseling." Ziggy, the cartoon character, put it differently, "the past is very important, it has a strong influence on your present and future - so you have to be very careful about what you have done in the past."

Carl Sandburg described the past as a bucket of ashes. Yet, many allow unpleasant events to smolder, putting themselves at risk of rekindling emotional bonfires. It seems to be a human tendency to want to change what has already happened. Accepting today as the last day of the first part of one's life is difficult for many to imagine. This guide will review reasons for such reluctance to let go of the past and then suggest some guidelines that offer encouragement to move forward with your life.

Often the desire to reverse history has to do with losses of relationships, ideals, or practical advantages. Whether it be a love relationship gone awry, discovering that as a parent you have lost out on what you believed child rearing was "supposed to" be about, being severed from long-term employment, or putting to better rest past abusive intrusions, most have much difficulty putting the grim facts of the matter behind. But the flow of life is forward. If you risk raking matters of the past over the coals once too often you may reheat yesterday's grievances, only to find out that they are spoiling your present.

Following are some reasons why, in spite of much time having elapsed, someone would cling emotionally to the adversity of the past as if the event had occurred recently:

1. *Grave digging to prove a point.* Tenaciously maintaining a grip on past happenings to prove that you were in the right - the "good guy" - and the other was in the wrong - the "bad guy" - only proves your fragile emotional nature in the face of your own flaws. Such defensive use of the past reflects an insecure state in which one would find oneself emotionally shattered if past mistakes were revealed.
2. *Axes to grind.* Reviving the past to open up old wounds so as to pour salt in them revives embittered tendencies. You may gain some immediate pleasure by expressing hostility for past injustices, but you end up reinforcing rather than extinguishing a bad habit.
3. *Magical thinking.* The thought that raking losses over the coals enough will cause the fire to go out is modern-day voodooism. Such superstitious thinking may prove to be disappointing. Believing that replaying your annoyances enough times will make them seem like nothing ever really happened may amplify what it is you wish to blot out. The more you practice thinking about something the more toward the forefront of your mind it is likely to remain.
4. *Promoting curiosity as an end in itself.* If you let it, curiosity can hinder attainment of your goals. Repeatedly going over past events with a fine-tooth comb, trying to determine the special "reasons" why events turned out as they did, can take on a life of its own. Sometimes this never-ending search to rework past details is seen as an answer to present problems, by searching for "insight" as to why things happened rather than simply accepting that they happened. This view, searching for the sake of searching, can lead to "paralysis of the analysis."

5. *Gaining others' pity.* Inviting others to feel sorry for you about your bad experiences is a childish form of attention getting. Vividly describing in depth details of former disadvantages gives away your wish for others to provide you with emotional pampering.
6. *Prove who had it worse.* Wallowing in murky descriptions of relationship and project failings can offer disturbed gratification and weak consolation for personal losses. Such indulgences make for deeper entrenchment in a past that won't change.
7. *Immediate convenience.* By focusing on what can't be changed, one gains a sense of relief, because the work required to override the past and gain a better result in the present can be avoided. Indulgence in the past serves as a distraction from prompt, sustained effort in the present - thus energy is saved by indulging in thoughts of days gone by. Immediate comfort is gained by resting yourself rather than testing yourself against up-to-date options.
8. *Fear of the unknown.* Humans bias themselves toward the familiar, however miserable it is. Some comfort, at least, is gained by remaining with a known quantity. This is the theme of the person who clings to the past: "Who knows what lies ahead in the sea of future uncertainty? It could be worse; it's best that one continue to struggle with the discomfort of the past."
9. *Dire needs for approval.* Revelation about one's past contrary experiences as a step to setting them aside does not always gain favorable responses from others. If you envision others gasping with disapproval about your revelations, and you make yourself anxious about such disapproval, you will likely avoid disclosing things about your past so as to avoid such slightings. Consequently, the openness that encourages forward movement is lost.
10. *Shame and guilt.* One does not have to bare one's soul totally to relieve tension from the past, but a moderate amount of transparency can help. Healthy public disclosure about former trespasses will be blocked if people believe (a) they could not shamefully tolerate public ridicule that might occur in the aftermath of social acknowledgement, or (b) they are to be damned and condemned

for their part in their handicapping experiences. This human tendency to personalize (e.g., "What's wrong with me that I couldn't control for more favorable experiences and then not be able to cope more suitably in the aftermath of my failings?") lies at the base of much ongoing emotional upset.

11. *Nostalgia addiction.* As bad as a time in one's life was, there may have been moments surrounding it that were tranquil and carefree. For instance, you may have been replaced in a love relationship but find the pleasant moments prior to your loved one's departure too tasty to resist giving less thought to. Continued indulgence in these longing fantasies about days gone by seems more gratifying than thoughts about dealing with the realities of the present. It may feel better to think of the past, but making yourself attached to these present comforts is detrimental to planning future possibilities. Living your life in rich fantasies of the past can bankrupt your future.
12. *To pass the buck.* Often, brooding about the past acts to transfer responsibility for misfortunes. For example, reworking how you believe your parents did you wrong permits you to defer accountability for your behavior to them. Such finger pointing is comforting in its own right; if others are to be held accountable for your behavior, you can conveniently work them over in your own mind rather than put forth the energy to get to work on paving a better way for yourself.
13. *Excitement-seeking tendencies.* One way to combat boredom is to rant and rave about former injustices. To stop structuring time with these dramatic measures would leave a vacuum in the day that may be seen as too difficult to fill.
14. *Fear of repeating failure.* Another rationalization for inaction comes from the belief that trying and failing again to realize one's values would be devastating and demeaning. Focusing on the horrors of past mistakes excuses any "risky" thoughts of another attempt at values realization.
15. *To white out blemishes.* Believing that it is necessary to wipe the slate clean by rearranging past circumstances in your mind until they fit more smoothly can motivate you

to harbor thoughts about these events. Such efforts try to deny that things were as bad as they were. By trying to paint a better picture of the past, one neglects facing up to the extent of the past problem.

The following suggestions offer some ways to unshackle the restraints of the past and move forward to bigger and better things:

1. *Understand the past to be a bridge to the present.* Your decisions and actions of the past got you to this point. Burning those bridges allows you to construct more hopeful methods of going on from here. Without wisdom gained from previous mistakes you will be unlikely to build a more enlightened future.
2. *Recognize the value of present-evidence decisions as opposed to right-or-wrong ones.* See that because you don't know tomorrow's answers today, there are no right or wrong choices, only decisions based on present evidence. It's best to accept the fact that you did the best you could with the information at hand at the time.
3. *Be glad you failed.* Many valuable lessons arise in the aftermath of poor judgment. With trial and error comes failure. Failure leads one to apply the process of elimination during the next effort. Learning from the school of hard knocks may not be a pleasant way to learn, but the lessons learned are likely to be remembered longer. Failure also shows that you believed in yourself enough to try on your own behalf and such efforts can be made to be habit forming.
4. *Itemize what you've learned.* Don't let the luxury of adversity get away without its benefits. Filter through your negative past experiences and sift out what can be to your advantage in the future. Sorting out the worst occurrence may reveal some of the best teachings.
5. *List the negatives.* Write out all that was bad from the relationship, position, or situation that was lost. Do so in a way that permits you to fully appreciate what you are not going to miss.
6. *Learn that prevention is more practical than cure.* After itemizing the adverse aspects of your loss, list some ways

and means you can use to avoid repeating those negatives. Clarifying "how not to do it" in the future can save much emotional wear and tear.

7. *Brainstorm.* Plot and scheme how you can gain in the present and future what you missed out on in the past. Fine-tune an alternate game plan that will inspire hope and increase the likelihood of your acquiring your wants in a different way.
8. *Utilize others' support and experience.* Profit from others' hindsight and coping abilities by networking with those who have experienced a similar fate as you. Join a support group or take an educational workshop where you can avail yourself of practical self-help information.
9. *Remove stimuli to memories.* "Out of sight, out of mind" has some truth to it. By setting aside reminders of your loss (e.g., pictures of a former mate, presents or other objects that recall previous experiences, etc.), you make it convenient to extinguish who and what you want to call to mind less. If you want to diet you can help yourself by removing high-caloric foods from your home. Likewise, if you want to partake less of the past, removing reminders that make it tempting to think about what can't be changed will help you to think more of what still can be.
10. *Produce present success.* One of the best remedies for the unfinished business of the past is success experiences in the present. Mop up yesterday's failures with today's successes. After some study, move on to another relationship, a different job, or an alternative belief system that has more promise of success.
11. *Change your view of time.* Picture the flow of life as being forward, and envision possibilities for the future. See that months or years down the road, what you are brooding about today may well appear as insignificant. By not mountain climbing over molehills today you will be better able eventually to set the past aside.
12. *Assume survival.* Understand that it's not a question of *if* you are going to survive difficult situations, but how much wear and tear you're going to give yourself in the meantime. Accepting survival as a foregone conclusion allows you to concentrate more on developing a more solid foundation for living in the present.

13. *Work against choice-blocking emotions.* Cut back on the following brands of emotional upset that keep the past alive:

    - *Anger.* Bittersweet revenge gained from harboring hostile thoughts will only boomerang and hurt you.
    - *Guilt.* Depreciating yourself due to your part in the mistaken plot will distract from future problem solving.
    - *Depression.* Feelings of hopelessness that are the result of protesting against a past that cannot be changed will further bind you and your present options.
    - *Shame.* Fear of public disclosure of your past mistakes blocks the transparency that might make it easier to move toward a more favorable mental health stance.
    - *Hurt.* This emotion that is the direct result of self-blame or self-pity invites you to pull back until the world is somehow made into a safer place to be.
    - *Fear.* Exaggerating past failures makes it easier to think of similar future possibilities as being more than shattering. Such dramatic views of potential failure excuses trying in the present.
    - *Self-Pity.* In addition to being a component of hurt, self-pity has a life of its own. Its existence in the form of whining and wallowing leads to the death of forward-looking options.

14. *Consider timing.* In calculating your present emotional management consider the following rule of thumb: The longer the time between the past happening and the present the more tapering down of emotions you can expect of yourself; the shorter the time that has elapsed since your loss the more intense your feelings are likely to be.
15. *Accept shades of gray.* To have feelings or not to have feelings about past intrusions is not the consideration. Understand your feelings to be not so much like a light switch as like a light dimmer. Rather than perfectionistically expecting yourself to turn feelings on and off like a

switch, see that as a human being you can dim or lessen, but not eliminate, them.

16. *Don't react to your reactions.* Don't startle yourself by your emotional leftovers. When you cause yourself to slip and experience intense emotions in the present as if it were the past, try not to upset yourself about feeling upset. Don't tell yourself: "What a terrible feeling. I can't bear feeling this way. What a foolish person I am for not being able to stand up against either my problem or my feelings about my problem." Instead, instruct yourself: "These feelings are sometimes difficult to cope with, but they are not extraordinary in the sense that I might let myself be overwhelmed by them. Emotional discomfort goes along with the territory of being human, and I'd best understand that reality to be within bearable, tolerable limits. I will try my best to stand up against my problems and emotional upset, but however far I might fall short of the mark in my coping, that would not be reason enough to condemn myself as a vile, sinister, putrid person."
17. *Don't awfulize.* It's not a question of *if* you think about past happenings but how often and how you explain these past facts to yourself. Think about your thinking, and see if you are not describing them as being beyond rather than a part of reality. To label experiences as "awful" is to give them surplus value, which will create surplus, unwanted emotions. Instead, use descriptions such as "bad," "difficult," "unpleasant," or "disappointing," which will better contain your emotional response.
18. *Recognize that problems exist in the present.* There is no such animal as a problem that isn't going on right now. To go back in time to detail the background of a current problem is to muddy the problem-solving waters. A historical search-and-destroy mission may rekindle some unpleasant features that you had long since forgotten.
19. *Avoid the company of misery.* Sometimes associates who know of or may have shared past unpleasantries will attempt to stimulate your interest in raking the past over the coals while stoking the emotions up one more time. Don't go for the bait. See that such instigations are a reflection of the agitators' own lack of meaning in life. Be-

cause they have nothing better to do than to attempt to smoke out trouble doesn't mean you have to go along with them.

20. *Use the ABCs of emotional reeducation.* Whether working against the primary problem of despising the facts of your misfortune or the secondary problem of despising yourself for not coping better with these facts, use the principles of rational thinking to get the upper hand on your emotions. Preferably, work on the secondary problem first as that will allow you to loosen yourself up about the fact that you give yourself a problem. Once you get yourself to lighten up about the reality of your coping skill deficiencies you will be better able to learn such skills.

The two charts on pages 61 to 64 illustrate this process. Begin by analyzing your coping skill deficiencies (see pp. 61-62). Now, with the problem about the problem under control, move on to the original overreaction (see pp. 63-64).

Both these examples illustrate the importance of understanding that the happenings at point A don't cause the feelings at point C. Rather it is the thoughts at B that more directly determine emotional outcome. Further, it is hopeful to realize that by practicing a different way of thinking at D, more favorable emotional effects can be gained at E. The rational-emotive method of problem solving as originated by Dr. Albert Ellis does not believe that people are not affected by life happenings, but that they affect themselves more than they are affected. This humanistic, antideterministic, more hopeful view of emotions believes that humans largely cause their own upset; that they influence themselves more than they are influenced. Consequently individuals do not have to wait for circumstances or individuals to change before feelings about such matters and persons can be changed.

Rational-emotive therapy (RET) emphasizes working against the secondary problem first. RET strongly suggests that you be more permissive with yourself; that you lighten up rather than tighten up about your fallible nature. It finds much value in taking pressure off yourself for having a primary problem prior to overcoming that original overreaction. As you stress yourself less about your shortcomings and overreact less to your initial overreactions, you put yourself more in control for curtailing them.

21. *Teach others.* One of the best ways to relearn a system of ideas is to present it to others. Explaining to associates the ABCs of emotional self-control as you wish to master them will reinforce the value of their application to your life.
22. *Sit right down and write yourself a letter* (but don't make believe it came from somebody else). Detail in writing the way you would like to unfold your future. Let your mind wander as to what these hopes might be. Calculate strategies that might get you over the hump of the present to the top of your future. Then, act the part of the person you described (yourself) in the days, weeks, months, and years ahead.
23. *Recognize that nothing works but working.* See that it's easier done than said. As difficult as you might think it is to take action, understand that it's even more difficult to maintain the status quo, which has no light at the end of its tunnel. Inspire hope by acknowledging that if you want something different to turn up it would be best to start by rolling up your sleeves.

In attempting to set yourself apart from an unwanted past you may not be able to avoid all the appearances of evil, but every little bit helps. Relinquishment of the past by remembering to remember to try to forget will not put you worlds apart from prior problems. However, such recall may provide for a happier existence in your world during the limited time you have in this world.

PART I - EMOTIONAL REEDUCATION ABOUT THE SECONDARY PROBLEM

A →	B →	C →	D →	E
(Activating event - what happened in manner of conduct)	(Beliefs, ideas, self-talk about flawed, deficient manner of emotional self-management in the aftermath of the original concern)	(Emotional consequences, feelings about coping faults)	(Strongly debate, dispute, take issue with initial beliefs)	(New effects)
Deficiencies in coping with a past negative event (i.e., high amount of emotional upset about lacking the ability to cope more constructively with the original problem).	"I should be handling my loss a lot better, if not be over it by now." "I have to get a handle on my emotions!" "How God-awful horrible that I'm still so upset!" "I'm bursting at the seams, I just can't put up with my discomforts and ineptitudes."	Guilt Depression Anxiety Self-hate and despisement Shame	"Where is it written that I am required by cosmic law to handle this matter any differently than I regretfully am? I wish I was presently more on the ball in gaining my wits about me but I, like anyone else, do not always do what is best - let me try and figure out how I can take more emotional control without agonizing about or putting myself down for my errors." "Is it noted someplace that my own discomfort about my disappointment or about	a. Changed philosophy - New, more open-minded way of looking at an old problem. Wish you were coping better but accept the fact you're not. b. Feel better and lighter - Sad but not depressed;

A →	B →	C →	D →	E
(Activating event - what happened in manner of conduct)	(Beliefs, ideas, self-talk about flawed, deficient manner of emotional self-management in the aftermath of the original concern)	(Emotional consequences, feelings about coping faults)	(Strongly debate, dispute, take issue with initial beliefs)	(New effects)
	"What a stinking rockhead I am for my shortcomings - damn me!"		others' disapproval in observing my failings is not tolerable? I doubt it! I can stand unpleasant feelings!"	regretful but not guilty; apprehensive but not anxious.
			"It's probably not that I'm not capable of better emotional self-management, it's just that I am unable to right now."	c. New behavioral effects - No time like the present to move forward with your life as you begin to consider more hopeful options.
			"Putting undue pressure on myself to get over my upset isn't going to help."	
			"Granted, my present method of handling my faults is stupid - but I'm not stupid. Damn my shortcomings, but not damn me."	

PART II - EMOTIONAL REEDUCATION ABOUT THE ORIGINAL OVERREACTION

A →	B →	C →	D →	E
(Activating event - original occurrence)	(Beliefs, self-talk about the loss, and what went wrong)	(Emotional consequences, feelings about disappointing event)	(Forcefully dispute initial way of thinking about the presenting problem)	(New effects)
Original loss (i.e., love relationship, job, etc.).	"This should never happen to anyone - especially me." "How unbearable this calamity is." "I cannot bear to live without what I value." "I hate what happened, I hate the person who caused	Depression Self-pity Anger Betrayal Shame	"Where is the evidence that these matters are not to occur in life? Apparently they do happen because they happened to me." "Can I document that I can't live without what I value? Likely not, in that I got along without what/who I lost long before I originally gained it/him or her." "People can select against	a. Changed philosophy - Think more clearheadedly and effectively while discovering new ways of looking at an old problem. b. Feel better - Disappointed

A →	B →	C →	D →	E
(Activating event - original occurrence)	(Beliefs, self-talk about the loss, and what went wrong)	(Emotional consequences, feelings about disappointing event)	(Forcefully dispute initial way of thinking about the presenting problem)	(New effects)
	this to happen, and I hate myself for letting it happen."		me. For me to think that others are not allowed to trespass against my values is undemocratic and does not match up with reality."	but not depressed; concerned but not consumed.
	"How ridiculous I am for not being able to control for what I value - I don't deserve to walk the face of this earth - I could never look other people in the eye again."		"Granted, I probably played a part in my own misfortune. This is par for the human course of things and because I am not superhuman I am not above such error proneness and I'd best not look down on myself for making mistakes."	c. New behavioral effects - Focus on correcting the fault rather than condemning self for having it.

Sound Alike, Look Alike, *Not* Alike: Alone Versus Lonesome

Evaluating whether people are content by the presence or absence of company in their life is judging a book by its cover. Like many things in life, outward appearances can be deceiving. Unfortunately, a human tendency is to jump to conclusions. When alone, especially for extended times, people tend to write off any potential happiness as a lost cause. However, being alone does not have to lead to lonesomeness. "What you see is what you get" is not necessarily true in the matter of personal happiness; what counts is what you *give yourself.*

David Reisman, in his book *The Lonely Crowd*, reflects that the loneliest people are often those surrounded by others. Likewise, many of the most contented people spend much time by themselves. There is much to be said for the contribution of solitude to emotional well-being. Whether loneliness supersedes contentment, or vice versa, depends on more than whether you are with someone else. Emotions are not at the service of social circumstances. What distinguishes these states, which on the surface appear as similar but yet are different, will be examined in this guide.

If you have recently left a close relationship and now find that you are required to structure much of your time by yourself; if your extended travels take you to territory without a familiar face in sight; if you have employment that assigns you a solitary role in the organization; if you didn't get invited to your office party even though you own the company; or if you are a member of a one-person band for whatever other reasons, the principles and methods reviewed here may assist you not only in avoiding loneliness but also in better appreciating and learning from your alone time.

Being at peace with oneself in the absence of a social group is both an art and a science. It requires creativity and imagination as well as the attainment of sound, scientific psychological principles. Directing your thinking beyond self, other, and cultural expectations is a key to overriding unwanted feeling states often assumed to be a part of being alone. Avoid putting yourself at the mercy of your dependency on others by considering the following suggestions:

1. *Avoid the self-fulfilling prophecy.* Don't trap yourself by convincing yourself of the foregone conclusion that you naturally will end up feeling unhappy when alone. Such preconceptions block other more hopeful options for attitudes and emotions. If you make a hard and fast pact with yourself to be lonesome when in an isolated situation you are likely to fulfill rather than dispute such an agreement.
2. *Distinguish normal from healthy.* A "normal" behavior is something that most people do. Such a consensus is often nothing to brag about. True, most people have a low tolerance for their own company and therefore often anguish themselves about being solo. However, such upset is not in line with the objectives of mental health. Try to do what is healthier for you rather than confine yourself to doing what is socially fashionable. Because most people might drive themselves stark raving unhappy about being alone doesn't mean you can't use your ingenuity and the psychological back-up discussed here to do otherwise.
3. *Track down and rip up preconceived ideas.* Humans need not act like trained seals, rats, or guinea pigs. The stimulus (S) does *not* cause the response (R). Humans do not react automatically to external stimuli. Between the S and the R is the organism (O), the person and his or her

notions that act as a go-between to link up the S and the R. Scrutinize your thinking closely for faulty ideas that you have about what being alone means for you. Honestly ask yourself if you don't semiautomatically kick into gear some of these premises when you are alone. Further, seek to determine whether it would be to your advantage to set aside such beliefs to see if they - and not the fact of your being alone - are the cause of your loneliness. Examples of such distress-producing beliefs are:

- "Others might see me by myself and think that I am unhappy and have no friends - and that would be shattering."
- "I feel nervous when I'm alone, and I can't stand feeling uncomfortable by myself."
- "I have to be with someone at all times because I'm so used to it. I couldn't bear doing something (like be by myself) if I'm not used to it."
- "I need someone to structure my time because I can't decide what to do with myself. If I was forced to decide I might make the wrong choice and then something terrible might happen - and that would be awful."
- "If people I know see me alone they might think I was up to something no good and then start bad rumors about me - and that would crush and disintegrate me totally."
- "What a schmuck I would make myself out to be if I couldn't get someone to accompany me."
- "I could never get used to being alone - it would be too hard and too useless to even try."
- "Would I ever be a jerk if I tried to be on my own more and failed to navigate well by myself. Others would say 'I told you so' and that would be humiliating."
- "I feel like a fish out of water when by myself. I can't stand the awkwardness and queasiness of it all. I have to get back in the comfort zone, that's all there is to it."

Replacing these "sad sack" ideas, which produce emotional disruption, with the following countering statements, might prove helpful in bridging the emotional gap while being apart from your social action:

- "True, others who see me alone might conclude that I am unhappily without friends. However, I am not required to pay their guesswork undue heed, and therefore I would do better to not overconcern myself with their hunches."
- "I often make myself nervous when by myself. This is not good, but it does not incriminate me as a human being. Let me see if I can figure out the ways and means to hassle myself less when alone while keeping in mind that in the meantime I can accept myself and withstand my symptom discomfort."
- "I'm used to being with people I know and I'll probably feel some uneasiness when alone. However, this getting used to is a small price to pay to learn how to depend more on the company of myself."
- "Granted, if I structure more time by myself I'll be required to make more of my own decisions. Especially at first I'll probably make more than my share of the wrong choices. But learning from my mistakes is part of how I will learn to become more of my own person."
- "Being alone is not all peaches and cream; but neither is participating with others. Nothing within a person or between people is ideal, and whether I'm alone or with others I would do better to focus on the advantages at the time."

4. *Develop a capacity to entertain yourself.* Solitude does not mean solitary confinement. The main confinement when being alone is making yourself a prisoner of your own thinking about how dastardly difficult it is to be by yourself and what to do with this individual time. Try not to restrict your time-structuring efforts to flicking on the stereo or being too quick to call someone to relieve your single dilemma. Instead, brainstorm potentially enjoyable options that require some planning and effort. One of the primary ingredients of mental health is the ca-

pacity to entertain yourself. Seize your alone time as an opportunity to develop this ability.

5. *Learn acceptance without resignation.* Acceptance includes the idea that "this is the way it is"; resignation tacks on "and this is the way it is always going to be." Acceptance is an active and hopeful view, while resignation is a more passive and fatalistic outlook. Accept the fact that you are alone, and then do something about it if you wish. Begin to strengthen your emotional capacity not only to survive but also to live and be happy by yourself.
6. *Opt for elegant solutions.* Perhaps the best time to actively seek companionship is when you have gotten to the point where you are comfortable by yourself, know you could continue to remain so indefinitely, but *choose* instead to get involved with another person. This higher level solution suggests that as much as you, like most humans, may prefer warmth and closeness, you'd best try not to turn such wants into demands. Relate to others by your choice and in your own time rather than in a driven, dependent manner.
7. *Avoid creating dramatic moments.* Don't exaggerate the significance of being without contact with others. Theoretically assuming the worst (e.g., "Wouldn't it be awful if I had to spend the weekend by myself!") will create advanced emotional upset that will feed on itself when the time alone eventually comes.
8. *Focus on the advantages.* Without the distraction of another's presence a fuller concentration on and appreciation of your activities can often be gained. For instance, eating a meal alone gives you the opportunity to enjoy each mouthful more than if you were following a conversation with someone else. Savings of time, energy, and money while accumulating a greater variety of experiences can be gained when not accommodating the motions of another. He or she who travels alone can travel faster, cheaper, with fewer delays, and with more breadth and depth of experience.
9. *Avoid sulking and self-pity.* Don't get hung up on yourself and the temptation to put yourself in your pity bucket. Such emotional wallowing is like a bottomless pit.

Indulgent thoughts such as "poor me," "woe is me," and "I've got it bad" will block a clearer view of what your options are when by yourself.

10. *Look at: Affected versus affect self.* It's not the shape of the road that more determines emotional outcome, but how you walk it. See that it's not aloneness that causes loneliness but what you're telling yourself as you walk down that solitary path. Energetically putting yourself in the driver's seat of emotional control may in itself provide a meaningful, special-interest companion.
11. *Appreciate vital absorptions.* Albert Einstein said that the best job for him would have been in a lighthouse. The Birdman of Alcatraz found much meaning in his study of birds even when isolated from society. Cultivating special interests or mastering unique projects can provide intense meaning to your existence that may well overshadow more temporary enjoyments that come from being with people. Such means of arriving at a satisfying state of mind are often more accessible than people-oriented activities.
12. *Use ignorance to advantage.* If you decide you want to make contact with others don't think that you have to know them or something about what they are talking about before you initiate or join in a conversation with them. Revealing ignorance is perhaps the best conversation starter. People usually like it when you ask them questions about something they are informed on but that you know little about. By first listening to others' specialized interests and aptitudes and then actively showing an interest in wanting to be informed about their knowledge, you begin to connect with them.
13. *Backtrack.* Think of times when you were alone and were pleasantly engaged in your activities. Borrow from the positive side of your track record to help regain composure in the present.
14. *Think of others.* Do a memory scan and think of those you have known who seemed to be by themselves a fair amount but appeared contented with their lot in life. Capitalize on their manner, conduct, style, and philosophies as you recall them. See if you can't model some of

these features to prevent your own aloneness from spilling over into loneliness.

15. *Display a pleasure menu.* List dozens of potentially enjoyable things you can do for yourself and by yourself that you could happily structure your time with. Keep this list in a strategic place in your residence where it will serve as a daily reminder of your options against solitary misery.
16. *Don't blame.* If you depreciate yourself for being unable to negotiate a present social standing you will make yourself guilty or depressed; if you blame others for not accommodating you with their presence you will make yourself angry; if you blame the conditions of life for not coming together with social provisions you will create emotional anguish of yet another vintage. In addition to the practical problem of being alone, by blaming you can give yourself a double or triple emotional whammy; this is several problems for the price of one - an offer you can and had best refuse.
17. *Don't brood - Do.* Ruminating on the fact of your being alone will only heat up your self-induced emotional turmoil. Turn to constructive, distracting activities to resolve your time-structuring concerns, which will cool down your emotional jets.
18. *Purposefully extend your alone time.* Stretch out the amount of time you spend by yourself. Each time you do this you document your ability to survive by yourself. Gradually building your emotional stamina in this way aspires hope for seeing yourself as an enjoying person in your own right.
19. *Use the scientific method.* Become a scientist in two ways:

    - *Get a data base.* Scientists start with a hypothesis. They then gather data that will support or refute their original belief. You too can test the validity of what you believe to be true. For instance, you may have several ideas such as "I can't stand being alone," or "If I made bad choices while by myself I'd be devastated and would then condemn myself for not being able to cope better." See if these ideas hold up against the scrutiny of scientific inquiry by spending some time by yourself at a time you would avoid doing so, for instance, on a weekend. If you die from the experience you prove your "I-can't-stand-it" theory. If you emerge the victor over your own aloneness, the theory is proven not to hold water.

- *Dispute.* Scientists debate or dispute their assumptions by asking "Where is the evidence?" "Where is the proof?" and "Can it be verified that these ideas are accurate?" Ideas can be disputed in words such as "Where is the evidence that I could not bear to be alone?" "Where is the proof that I would be a stumble bum of a human being if I coped poorly with my aloneness?" Looking at these two examples, one can see the falsehood that runs through them. This is because anything is bearable as long as you're alive; therefore this dramatic view is more than a slight exaggeration. Also, there is no proof that if you acted inferior in the throes of being by yourself that this would mean you were forever and always an inferior being.

Beliefs can also be disputed with behavior. Acting against these same crooked notions allows you to dispute and disprove their truth in a hands-on manner. Experiencing an atypical extended time by yourself permits you to see what's what, apart from your earlier hunches. Finally, ideas can be disputed with your emotions. Substituting a different emotion during the experience of being alone will make that time by yourself more tolerable, if not enjoyable. Train yourself to think and act in ways that promote concern without anxiety; sadness without depression; annoyance without anger; regret without guilt. This can help pave the way for more desirable feelings of happiness, joy, and elation.

When you anticipate being alone, dispute at all three levels - thinking, behavior, and emotions - to provide a three-pronged attack at overcoming your loneliness stalemate. Furthermore, the *sooner* you get after your problem, the *stronger* you dispute your concerns, and the *longer* you stay with these three debating methods, the *better* emotional results you are likely to get. Although it is not true that you will never walk alone, it is likely that if you play your attitudinal, behavioral, and emotional cards right as you walk alone you will seldom be miserable. In fact, as you apply and refine some of the suggestions given here you may well go full circle and gain the higher level solution of appreciating the advantages of aloneness by choice as opposed to fretting about being alone by chance.

Complacency: Roots, Rudiments, And Remedies

Humans seem to take themselves so far and no further in their personal development. They appear to want more to make what's bad okay than to make what's okay better. In love, vocation, and health care, as well as other ambitions that contribute to their happiness and survival, most allow deterioration of gains made to set in. Lifestyle matters of health and happiness are seen as a place one gets to and automatically stays at rather than something that requires regular upkeep. Advantages are lost because holding one's own is seen as a downhill flow rather than an uphill battle. This guide will examine why people more often than not push themselves back into bad habits rather than build further on gains made. Then, suggestions for overcoming this nonchalant, take-for-granted tendency will be given.

People bring themselves to their behavior by what they suggest to themselves about what keeping a good thing going means for them. Gains slip away when holding to the faulty idea that "I've worked hard to get to where I want to be - therefore I shouldn't be required to keep my nose to the problem-solving grindstone to maintain these advantages that I have worked oh-so-hard to obtain." Pretending that good results will automatically extend themselves blocks the effort that got you to where you wanted to be to begin with. There is no universal backup generator that will continue to move you forward with the accomplishments you've arrived at. There are other variations of loosely knit thinking that lead to resting on one's laurels. Few seem to thrive on meeting the challenge of nourishing dividends by keeping interest high because they instead indulge in the following:

1. *"Sweet lemon" reasoning.* Pretending that the lemon tastes sweet and that therefore you like what you have allows you to easily change your game plan before the game is won. If you like what you have you can easily escape the hard work required to go further with results to date. By putting your efforts in neutral you avoid the hassles of moving forward without considering the advantages of future benefits.
2. *Pipe dream thinking.* Believing that planning makes it so and that a thinking decision is the same as a doing decision creates a lulling effect. This leaves plans as an end in themselves rather than as a means to an ongoing end. When schemes are given a life of their own, apart from the action component, gains made are likely to die on the vine.
3. *Loopholes in one's philosophy of effort.* After getting past the attitude "It's too hard to begin," this exaggerated belief about effort goes out the back door only to be brought in the front door under the guise of: "It's too hard to keep up the beat over the course of a lifetime." It is true that concentrated effort to keep in place goals that have been attained is hard, and perhaps the extended energy required to keep things going is more than is required to get it going in the first place. But excessively stating that it is just "too hard" makes it very convenient to believe that because of the abundant amount of upkeep required, one is beat before one starts - so why start?
4. *Loopholes in a philosophy of reciprocation.* Struggling to get to a point of satisfaction in life is one thing; expecting life to for always and ever cater to us because of these dues paid is another. Little comes easily but trouble and calories. Gaining satisfaction is a process rather than a permanent state, and the perspiration needed for such an indefinite project had best be accepted as a part

of the process of self-development. Rather than "It's too tough to keep it up," better by-words would be: "Tough if I'm required to not only roll up my sleeves and go to work but also to keep them rolled up if I am to gain and hang on to the advantages that add meaning to my life."

5. *Comfort trappings*. Smugness sets in when the immediate comforts of success are allowed to override the long-range satisfactions of upkeep. Loss of vital absorption allows unsustained effort to dominate.
6. *One-in-the-hand-is-worth-two-in-the-bush views*. Being happy with what you have is important. Recognize that life is ever-changing and that if you don't adapt to these changes you risk being left in the dust. The "one in the hand" may provide some security, but the "two in the bush" provide a ready reserve if you lose your grip on the former.
7. *Conflict avoidance*. Going only so far may not catch the contrary attention of too many people. Going further may result in public disclosure, which makes you subject to the possibility of rubbing more people the wrong way. "This is good enough; if I make it better others might hassle me - and I couldn't tolerate that" is an attitude that maintains the status quo.
8. *Fear of failure*. Having succeeded at getting as far as they have some do not wish to press their "luck" by going further. The idea that "If things have gone your way, watch out because bad things are likely to happen if you try to advance further" often disguises a fear of failure. "If I try to carry the ball further I might fail, and if I fail I'd be a louse, so I'll avoid failure and lousehood by not trying" is the kind of statement that promotes the choice of leaving well enough alone rather than nourishing it to make it better.
9. *Disapproval anxiety*. Thinking that if you complete the task others may not approve of the finished product will discourage you from refining the loose ends. Believing that if less attention is paid you you will be subject to less criticism camouflages people-pleasing tendencies that encourage project efforts to remain "as is."
10. *Fear of success*. Believing that once you establish your ongoing capabilities others are likely to place even higher

expectations on you can encourage a leveling off of achievement goals if those added expectations are seen as drudgery that you would just as soon avoid. Fewer expectations are placed on the challenging underdog than on the incumbent; perhaps such added pressure is extra baggage that you would just as soon do without.

11. *"Sour grapes" thinking.* By convincing yourself that the next rung on the success ladder - or just maintaining yourself at the level attained - isn't so great to begin with, a philosophy of "Why try harder?" is quickly established. The possibility that you won't like what you don't yet have - and the realization of the extra effort it will take to get it - leads to an attitude of "That something extra is probably sour anyway."
12. *Guilt.* Not wanting to appear "too successful," because you would down yourself for giving off the impression of thinking you are better than others, creates a false sense of humility, which blocks adding onto gains made. Judging yourself by any appearance of "uppityness" keeps you low on the ladder of achieving your ambitions.
13. *Prolonged fantasy and underreactiveness.* Thinking that gaining and maintaining your project is "simple," "easy," "a snap," and could be done in the twinkling of an eye, "if I really wanted to" provides enough of a gratification in fantasy that it seems hardly worth the effort to create a similar experience in reality.
14. *Self-pity.* Feeling sorry for yourself for efforts put forth to date is encouragement to yourself to pull back from continued energy output. "Poor me" will get poor results in extending behaviors in line with your best interests.
15. *Belief in a quick fix.* After shooting your wad and getting good results, fooling yourself into believing that fallout momentum will magically take care of itself will result in another stalemate entrenchment. Staying with the program bows to the immediate frenzy associated with a first time, all-out effort. Initial exaggerated effort is seen as an end in itself rather than a first step in a gradual but sure self-help process.
16. *Relative level of anxiety.* Thinking that once the crisis is past one can coast can be a problem. Believing that one is required to be in a state of high-level crisis with the

motivational anxiety that goes along with such a peak experience is the opposite side of the choice-blocking coin. If one can only problem solve when in a heightened and frightened state of mind this leaves much time in the day inaccessible to the requirements of motivational upkeep.

17. *Deprivation anxiety.* Thinking that your cup of what you consider acceptable deprivation already runneth over, and that any more going without would be "unbearable," will bring to a halt the persistence necessary to carry on further.
18. *Stubbornness, pigheadedness, and bullheadedness.* Insisting that any further inconveniences not exist and refusing to accept the fact of their existence results in a spinning of your wheels. Judging consistent inconvenience to be bigger than life results in getting yourself caught up in protesting against the alleged awesomeness of the continued task. This protest often comes in the form of a "should" statement, for instance, "This project has been hard enough already. Enough is enough! It shouldn't remain so hard, and I shouldn't have to be inconvenienced any further!"
19. *Fear of uncertainty.* Commanding that before you go further with your efforts you require tomorrow's answers today will cause you to run out of steam before your enterprise is complete. Such a paralysis of the analysis that comes from insisting on a complete inventory of all outcome possibilities prior to forging ahead will lock you into a philosophy that curiosity is an end in itself.
20. *Dependence on others.* Making yourself dependent on others' continued cooperation is another way to mark time. Thinking that you need help to carry the ball further puts you at the mercy of others' willingness to assist. Such dependent tendencies put you out on a limb when the going gets tough and there is nobody around to help.
21. *Pity for others.* Feeling sorry for others and working overtime to help them leaves you with little time to stabilize and build from your own projects.
22. *Human shifting and drifting.* Humans tend to go in the direction they are headed. If they do the right thing for a period of time but briefly slip off track they are more

than likely to take this slip and turn it into a major setback. This simple fact of life often goes unnoticed in explaining how people get themselves off the beaten track of self-interested behaviors.

It is one thing to describe reasons for problems. It is another to prescribe constructive options. Although it seems a natural tendency to mark time en route to a fuller life, such stalling tendencies need not be made binding. The following suggestions may prove helpful in not derailing yourself from your chosen path of extended happiness.

1. *Develop rational slogans.* Ideas such as the following will assist in keeping yourself alert and on target toward completion of the project: "Doing gets it done." "Nothing works but working." "It's not easy to take the easy way out." "The line of least resistance is often the line of most resistance." "Inspiration comes from perspiration." "Present pain for future gain." "No time like the present."
2. *Decide to pay now or pay later.* As hard as it is to keep up the beat in following along further, it's harder not to. Ask yourself: "Do I want to feel better now (by not extending myself and dropping the matter), or do I want to feel better for the rest of my life (by gaining and maintaining what contributes to my health and happiness)?"
3. *Develop a relapse prevention method.* If you push yourself off the wagon of success you can quickly pull yourself back on. By seeing that all is not lost when you err you can prevent repetition of your mistake.
4. *Realize that prevention is better than cure.* Believing that you don't have to be sick to get better will propel you further in doing what's best for you. By stretching your efforts now you will be preventing problems later; knowing this will help you to ward off larger problems down the road.
5. *Monitor yourself honestly.* Regularly review the fruits of your labor and honestly assess your good intentions to make sure they are backed by the right methods; this will better assure that you won't stop yourself short of the mark.

6. *Check with an unbiased consultant.* To make sure that you are sailing along as well as you think you can, get objective feedback about your progress: check with the bathroom scale if you believe you are meeting the requirements of losing weight; have a nurse take your blood pressure if you think you have changed your lifestyle enough to lower your blood pressure; confer with your teacher if you believe that your current study habits are leading to greater academic excellence than your previous habits.
7. *Motivate yourself by deliberation rather than desperation.* See that you don't have to put yourself into a crisis before you expand efforts on your own behalf. Understand that making yourself frantic is not the only or best means of keeping yourself in gear. Instead, take a long-range view of life and focus on the future advantages of completing what you started.
8. *Focus on process more than outcome.* Try to see your efforts as having a life of their own. Trying on your own behalf can have value in itself. By focusing on what you are doing rather than how well you are doing or on what other people might be thinking about your efforts you avoid distractions from the business at hand.
9. *Get rid of undue reciprocity expectations.* Accept that even your best efforts aren't required to be returned in kind. The universe doesn't have to reward your toil with success. Others don't have to support or appreciate your solid efforts. Getting rid of these dependency ties deflates tension, freeing up energy that can be put to use in finishing what you started on your own.
10. *Distinguish between feeling better and getting better.* It feels good to get a running start on your projects, but basic changes aren't made until you finish the race. A false sense of well-being gained from dabbling in an enterprise is a poor substitute from satisfactions gained from more complete reorganization.
11. *Sort out wants from needs.* When you make yourself independent of success, approval, cooperation, and other supposed necessities you will be better able to forge ahead in a more clearheaded manner with your goals. Such external props are matters of convenience but are

not all-important. Rationally understanding that you're better off not making yourself require what you want will result in less hesitation more often.

Getting a program of self-help off the ground and keeping it in the air are two different things. Sidetracking can be remedied by avoiding the comfort trap of partial success. Take motivational matters into your own hands by seeing that nothing but doing is likely to get the job done. Motivate yourself to follow it through from beginning to end, with no stalling tactics in between, and you'll be traveling a wiser route than that of complacency.

Will Lack of Undying Understanding Really Kill You?

Understanding is one of those rare commodities that many are interested in getting but most aren't very willing to give. Many cry out for this form of recognition comfort, but few experience it. Three little words - "I understand you" - exist as a near vacuum in most people's lives; this is perhaps the most commonly overlooked communication that humans give themselves problems about. Taking too seriously the importance of being understood lies at the base of unwanted feelings of hurt, anger, betrayal, self-pity, fear, and anxiety. If lack of understanding is often the rule rather than the exception for you, this guide presents information about how not to let such disappointment get under your skin.

Short of getting down on yourself or angry at others for their empathic negligence, what can be done to oversee and emotionally rustproof your response to such neglect? The following standard operating procedures in the face of lack of understanding (and closely related concerns about gaps in others' cooperation, consideration, acceptance, and approval) can help you learn how to overreact less and accept yourself more in spite of such lapses.

1. *Acknowledge your dependency and meet it head on.* Admit that you sometimes tend to see other's understand-

ing of your feelings and opinions as sacred. Then, don't put yourself down for your fault; see that because someone understands you poorly (a) it isn't the end of the world, and (b) it does not discredit you in any way.

2. *Don't crave.* Avoid lusting after never-ending understanding and approval. Distinguish between want and need. See that others' understanding of the what and the who in your message is nice but not necessary; important but not urgent.
3. *Don't get defensive.* Don't think you are required to justify why your views contrast with what the other person believes to be correct. A false sense of obligation appears as if you are at the mercy of and beholding to the other person.
4. *Remember, you're not on trial.* Whether the other person understands, agrees, or cooperates does not stand you in judgment by the other's standards. Attempting to prove your innocence when you're not guilty of anything to begin with will make you the plaything of others' applause.
5. *Don't overexplain.* No matter what you say, if you find that it's not what the other wants to hear, save your breath. You're not going to sell people a used car they don't want, or teach them something they don't want to learn. Overexplaining will result in you making yourself frustrated from trying to reason people out of something they haven't been reasoned into.
6. *Don't apologize for yourself.* Practicing the nauseating humility of licking others' feet simply because you can't penetrate their understanding subtracts from the bargaining power, the give and take, that balanced relationships are made of.
7. *Don't plead.* Frantic efforts to garner your assumed requirements for understanding put you in a one-down, one-sided, no-win position. A sure way to drown is to petrify yourself about the possibility of not being able to swim.
8. *Don't perfume or deny.* Trying to make it look like there really isn't a difference of opinion when there is is a futile attempt to conceal the obvious reality that two people aren't always going to be on the same wavelength.

9. *Don't threaten.* Making yourself angry at the other for not understanding you is yet another counterproductive means of approaching another's unfavorable response to you. Such finger pointing will result in others being less inclined to associate with you, to say nothing about understanding you.
10. *Watch the enthusiasm.* In the afterglow of someone meeting you halfway, if you pour it on too thick (i.e., "*I really appreciate* your understanding") you'll be giving off the message that, because their likings are ultra-important for you, you will therefore be miserable without such future approval. This message sets the stage for the other to be tempted to take advantage of your dependency.
11. *Don't attribute magic.* Others' understanding does not validate you, affirm you, or turn you into a special person. Rather, such gentle granting of acceptance means that you have market value with others in that their tastes and preferences are compatible with the unique attitude and behavior offerings that you bring to the relationship.
12. *Cut down on the practical disadvantages.* Give yourself other options as you consider the practical clout someone might wield in your life. For instance, if your boss could misunderstand or disapprove of your performance to the point of dismissing you, research other job possibilities in case that happens. Or, if you're a partner in a marriage where your mate's disapproval of your actions might lead to him or her seeking a divorce, brainstorm ways to become more financially self-sufficient. Having this type of "ace in the hole" makes it more convenient for you to be your own person - with or without the other's understanding.
13. *Understand yourself.* Knowing what you truly want out of life and actively following your natural bents allows you to rely less on others for this knowledge and understanding.
14. *Accept yourself.* Accepting yourself for no special reason, and whether other's views are favorable or unfavorable, breaks the tie that binds you to others' whims and opinions about you.

15. *Count on yourself.* One of the few things in life that there is no extra charge for is relying on yours truly. Develop confidence to go on with your life with or without others' unending encouragement. Strive steadily for what is important to you.
16. *Face the music.* Make an open position statement about what you view to be a misunderstanding. Tell the other person what you view to be the gap in understanding - without telling him or her off. Then. . . .
17. *Restate once.* When faced with misunderstanding, briefly restate and clarify your position - preferably no more than once. Beyond this, your best efforts to get through what may be the other person's thick skull are likely to fall on deaf ears. Perhaps, no matter what you say, it's not what the other person wants to hear.
18. *Practice understanding others.* One of the best ways to gain understanding from others is to give it. Train yourself to become an active sounding board not only of the content of what others say, but also their feelings. Empathy training by "walking a mile in your associate's moccasins" is likely to increase the degree of understanding directed your way.
19. *Track down your irrational ideas.* You can become more your own person by detecting faulty notions that produce your yearnings. Beliefs such as "I have to be sure I get him to understand me," "It's terrible when I don't get through to him," "I can't stand being on the outside looking in for favoritism," and "If I'm badly misunderstood, then I'm bad" had best be screened for their contributions to your upset.
20. *Vigorously dispute, debate, and argue against your irrational beliefs.* Create a different way of thinking about what others' accommodations mean for you. Build a case for emotional self-control and self-acceptance by challenging your original false assumptions. Ask yourself: "Where is the evidence that I require another's understanding, acceptance, approval, or cooperation? Such niceties would be just that - nice but not necessary!" "Why would it be terrible if I didn't puncture another's dislikes, and is there really any proof that I couldn't stand such negligence to buy into my way of thinking?" "How

would another's taking me wrong represent me as bad?" "What's more important: how others understand and accept me, or how well I understand and accept myself?"

Try and see that others' ongoing understanding, continually tuning into your values, or being exceedingly accepting of you are some of the many good things in life that you don't have to have. Make the distinction between the infrequency of others' support and your upset about it, and see that one doesn't have to follow the other. Life is too short to hang on to a lifeline that isn't required; you can learn how to swim alone.

Happiness as Paradox: Expecting Less and Getting More

Mental health is a lot like dental health - everybody has a few cavities. No one experiences constant happiness. Imperfect people in an imperfect world is the rule, not the exception. Emotional stability is not the absence of problems. All humans are born with tendencies toward upset and disturbance, although some make themselves more upset than others. It is important for one's emotional well-being not to get caught up in the "perfect person syndrome."

The central theme of this guide is to encourage a decent respect for - though not an intimidation of - human limits. Because humans and their life circumstances *could be* less limited than they are doesn't mean that they *have to be* any less restrictive than they are. Undamning acceptance that matters are presently the way they are, and "so be it," is a primary ingredient toward molding one's mental health.

Happiness is a slippery, elusive, fleeting item at best and is a relative by-product of what one expects. There is often a difference between what seems reasonable and what really exists. Distinguishing the reality from the dream, and gracefully lumping the gap between the world as you would like it to be in your head and as it actually exists is a key to happier living.

Realizing that the sky *isn't* the limit while trying to attain one's fuller potential can be done by shooting for three bull's-eyes of acceptance: self, others, and life. Happiness can be seen as a direct ratio between what you *expect* of self, others, and the conditions of life and what you *get* from these same three factors. Shooting for these targets of emotional well-being doesn't mean you will hit the bull's-eye every time, but because you have a bead on such ideals, probably you will come closer to them and hit them more often than if you hadn't identified such objectives. Let's examine these three target areas more closely and see how mastering a clear-headed view of them can assist in gaining more happiness.

ACCEPTANCE OF SELF

What people frequently expect of themselves is perfection; what they get is something far less - fallibility. The notion that you are required to do perfectly well or else you're perfectly worthless contradicts emotional well-being and leads to unwanted feelings of depression, guilt, anxiety, fear, and shame. Complicating matters further, to wrongly believe you must be perfect at not experiencing these unpleasant feelings will give you a problem about your problem - two problems for the price of one: (a) your undesirable feeling, and (b) your self-downing for having the feeling.

Some things in life cannot be forced. You can't force yourself to relax - you allow yourself to do so. You can't force yourself to be happy - you allow yourself this experience by accepting your flaws as part of being human. Take pressure off yourself. Lighten up rather than tighten up about your faults - including not being able to gain control over your undesirable emotions. This will bring your emotions more in line with the state of mind you wish to experience more often. Learning to co-exist with emotional cavities is perhaps the highest level solution to emotional upset. Holding a handful of sand and squeezing tightly will lose much of it, while loosening your grip will retain more of it. So too, forcing the impossible issue of insisting on perfection will result in losing more of the happiness you would like to attain.

ACCEPTANCE OF OTHERS

More often than not, what is expected of others is kind and fair treatment. What is usually obtained is a lesser experience called ordinary or normal neglect. Those whom we care about the most are likely to treat us caringly with disappointing infrequency. This is because others have their own concerns to settle on. Even when what you are expecting seems reasonable, when another person consistently doesn't deliver what you anticipate from him or her, you are expecting too much. Whether the other's limitations be due to motivation, ignorance, or disturbance, your expected requirements are beyond his or her capacity.

To close this gap between what you're expecting and what you're getting you probably will be required to expect less. Abandoning the wishful thinking that accompanies attempts to change another human being releases the pressure of trying to do the impossible. Going from "Be reasonable; do it my way" to "I'll be reasonable as you do it your way" will likely result in directing more peace of mind in your own direction.

ACCEPTANCE OF LIFE

What is expected of life and the universe is that it be made easier for you to obtain fulfillment and reach your goals. When such pipe-dream anticipations fall short of the mark, what often is made to follow is whining, procrastination, and self-pity. The idea that you can use such mannerisms to get even with life for not conveniencing you is akin to "cutting off your nose to spite your face."

This does not mean that accepting life's conditions as they exist means lying down and dying while letting people and matters of concern take advantage of you. Trying to make the world bend for the pleasure of your values is one thing, but ranting and raving if such efforts fail is another. Do what you can to change what you can while protecting yourself from what you can't. When you stamp your feet when a return on your investment doesn't occur, you forget about protecting yourself from your own emotional discharges.

When conditions of life and the people in it hold you in unfair disfavor, this is all the more reason to be fairer to yourself. Every obstacle in life that exists - be it self, other, or chance factor created - is required to exist; because it does. There is no reason why anything is mandated to be anything other than it is. Denying reality and protesting against unpleasantness reflects crooked thinking that demands something or somebody should (must, has to, ought to, is supposed to) be different than they actually are.

It is unlikely that any human will become the ultimate ideal specimen of indefinite happiness. Yet, progress in self-development can be made. Try asking and answering three basic questions in a way that will make it convenient for you to expect less and get more emotional fulfillment.

1. *Question Number 1:* "What do I really need or require; what is essential, a prerequisite for my life; what do I really have to have?"
   Answer: "Though I want and even wish for many things in life - such as high-level performances, a good number of accomplishments, and the acceptance and approval of a majority of those that I judge to be significant to me - none of these are absolute requirements. In fact, it is my desiring, hoping, and striving for these advantages that adds much meaning to my existence, for I realize that to never be sad or disappointed in life would require me to evacuate my values - and I sure don't want to go through my life experience without meaning. In short, I very persistently and perseveringly want certain things as vital parts of my life - but I don't have to have what I want; I would do well for my personal happiness to not necessitize the niceties of living."
2. *Question Number 2:* "What can others really do to me, especially those I truly care about?"
   Answer: "Others can frustrate, deprive, inconvenience, or dissatisfy me by not making the provisions I hoped for from them. They can also select and discriminate against things that they don't like about me. However, because, as far as I know, there is no magic to words, they cannot hurt, depress, or anger me. 'Sticks and stones will break my bones but words will never harm me' - unless I sharpen them up and stick them in myself. Neither can others put me down, demean me, or discredit me - only I can do that by believing that others' bad opinions of me equal me. When others' tastes and preferences clash with what I have to offer, it tells me a lot about them - but nothing about me. If I accept myself, others' not accepting me

can't touch me emotionally." As Eleanor Roosevelt said, "No one can make you feel inferior without your consent."

3. *Question Number 3:* "What does life and the world really owe me?"
   Answer: "There is no evidence that supposed cosmic forces owe me anything. I'd best not lead myself to believe that I am the one person in the universe who has to get his or her way all the time, or be treated fairly all or any of the time. Such immature thinking is likely to get me nowhere fast. As much as I may want partiality in gaining certainty and orderliness in a world where there seem to be no such animals, I'd better accept that this or anything else that my little heart desires is not due me. No matter how many dues I might see myself paying, there is no proof that I am entitled to the things that I miss, including eternal bliss. All the griping, moaning, and groaning that I can muster isn't going to make poor me any better off. The world doesn't have to be partial toward me - tough!"

What do you really need in life? What can others really do to you? What does the world really owe you? If you (a) answer all three with "nothing," and (b) back that answer up with supportive evidence similar to the statements provided here, you will, by reducing your expectations of self, others, and life, give yourself a head start toward helping yourself to feel happier, more often, for longer periods of time.

Intrusive Events as the Red Herring of Emotional Disturbance: Fine-Tuning Human "Upset-Ability"

I recently counseled with a 5-year-old young lady who had the misfortune of being sexually abused by her alcoholic father. I asked her: "What does it mean for you that your father touched your private parts?" She responded, "It means Daddy's got problems." Her position reflects the intention of this guide: Just because people have feelings about an event does not mean that the event caused the feelings; that the feelings we experience while in a circumstance are subject to our interpretation of the event. My young client had perspective on her misfortune. She wasn't overreacting to or personalizing it. She was able to see that the incident showed her father's disturbance rather than wrongly assuming it reflected something about her.

When neglectful or abusive circumstances occur, it's often taken for granted that the outcome will be disturbance; this view becomes a self-fulfilling prophecy. Due to tendencies toward suggestibility, recipients of such experiences are expected (and expect themselves) to take on marked emotional disturbance. For instance, it is nearly un-American to be an adult child of an alcoholic parent and not have significant upset.

In near-fanatical proportions, scare tactics are used to convince people that they have problems they never knew they had. This is akin to looking for a needle in a haystack and, when none is found, quickly putting one there, claiming it was there all the while. Pushing people into molds that don't exist is a tunnel-visioned approach to emotional problem solving. The message is often given that if you were involuntarily subjected to circumstances against your will, you have to develop serious emotional complications from such adversity. In sorting out the roots of emotional problems the implications often are that (a) when you have certain intrusive experiences you are naturally going to take on and maintain a high level of upset about such matters, and (b) if you hadn't had such intense experiences you wouldn't presently have such emotional handicaps.

The view presented here holds that such assumptions are misguided when trying to figure out (a) how humans disturb themselves, and (b) what they can more quickly do to lessen such disturbances.

In reality, humans are born remarkably fallible. They have emotional problems for no special reason other than the fact that they are human. Humans overreact to problems, and the bigger the problem, the more likely they are to blow it out of proportion. In short, all humans seem to bring into the world a bias toward "upset-ability" - the ability to upset themselves. Their upset-ability is brought *to* the family or other "dysfunctional" situation rather than being *caused by* it.

Humans deal with problems of a particular life circumstance the same way they deal with problems generally. If it hadn't been convenient to disturb themselves in the difficult situation at hand, they would simply do so in another context. In short, humans are emotional "basket cases" first and family and societal members second.

Although no problem is so small that it can't be blown out of proportion, individuals are selective about which molehills they make into mountains. Emotional disturbance is part of a more general disturbed philosophy of living that is seen in tendencies toward:

1. *Overgeneralization:* "If I fail, I'm a failure."
2. *Exaggeration:* "It couldn't be any worse."
3. *Overreaction:* "This is terrible and I can't stand it."

4. *Personalization or self-depreciation:* "What's wrong with me that I'm not able to get him or her to treat me better?"
5. *Perfectionism:* "I have to do better than anyone else and better than the last time I did it."
6. *Demandingness:* "I'm the one person in the universe who has to get his own way all the time - my will be done!"
7. *Downingness:* "When I act badly, I'm bad." "When others act badly they're bad." "When the universe doesn't cater to me it stinks."

Whether raised in a good or bad environment, and regardless of their social circumstances, humans seem inclined toward these tendencies. To overlook the obvious is to camouflage the rudiments of emotional problems and wrongly pin the cause of the upset on external events. Such cause-and-effect thinking puts sufferers at the mercy of their environment and minimizes their chances of taking a stand against life's conditions. These tendencies toward disturbance are powerful, but they do not have to override the individual in his or her situation - regardless of severity. Understanding this provides a running start toward greater emotional self-control. To see that you affect yourself more than you are affected removes the culprit of emotional disturbance from unwanted events. To muddy this reality distracts from a clearer problem-solving focus.

Emotional disturbance is not like the common cold; it's not a virus that you can catch. People are not passive recipients of their emotional problems. There is no magic that automatically hands people feelings along with their experiences. If happenings caused feelings then the same happening would cause the same feeling in everyone. To think that intrusive realities cause emotional realities is to go against the grain of human potential - the ever-present human possibility to *not* buckle under in an overreactive, self-blaming way.

Think back on some of the worst things that ever happened in your life and try to see them as just that and nothing more. They were some of the worst experiences you could ever have, and they were an unpleasant part of your life, but they are not bigger than your life. Try to use some of the following suggestions to avoid taking a bad experience and amplifying its importance in the scheme of your life; to more clearheadedly sort out, and even use for your future advantage, what you learned from such happenings.

1. *Change preconceived ideas.* Most people have their minds made up about what certain situations would mean for them. Then, when these circumstances arise, these self-concocted ideas are semiautomatically kicked into gear. Reexamine self-statements such as "That was awful, I can't bear to think about it" (multiplies the discomfort); "If I were a better person I would be able to cope with this better" (self-depreciation); and "This never should have happened" (denial of reality). Challenge these statements with new ones, such as "That was one of the most difficult, yet bearable happenings in my life" (sets boundaries on discomfort); "I wish I were coping with this better because I would be better off, but the fact that I'm not doesn't make me a worse person" (promotes self-acceptance); and "I wish this had never happened but it did - so be it" (acceptance of reality).
2. *Tear up society's blueprint.* Strive for rational nonconformity by not buying into cultural expectations about how you "should," "must," or "have to" act given certain adversity. If you were victimized early in life, it isn't required that you pyramid these instances by keeping alive original reactions. For example, in our society if you have been abused you are naturally expected to carry forth a large amount of hurt, hate, and fear. See that you can be *in* the world without being *of* the world in terms of expected long-term emotional fallout.
3. *Don't judge yourself.* Having been exposed to bad experiences doesn't make you bad. Your perpetrator's bad problems don't reflect on you but rather on his or her disturbance.
4. *Don't judge the other.* If you rate yourself as bad you're likely to make yourself feel guilty or depressed; if you rate the other as bad you are likely to make yourself angry or vindictive. Do yourself a favor and take yourself off such an emotional roller-coaster.
5. *Confront the perpetrator.* When possible, let the other know how his or her taking advantage of you in remov-

ing your freedom of choice was a difficult event for you to deal with. In no-nonsense fashion tell him or her that it is no thanks to him or her that you have been able to get as far in your personal development as you have.

6. *Be transparent.* Opening up to others about your bad experiences helps to counter any shame you might have in the aftermath of these significant events.
7. *Put lessons to good use.* Do your best to examine the doughnut as well as the hole in the doughnut. Honestly looking back on the worst experiences you have ever had may result in identifying those teachings that in the long run contributed to your well-roundedness as a human being.
8. *Talk with others in the same boat.* Albert Schweitzer once remarked on the special kinship that exists among those who "bear the mark of pain." Realizing that you're not alone in your misfortune is another factor that can contribute to your lightening up rather than tightening up.
9. *Don't avoid taking risks.* Mark Twain's cat jumped on a hot stove and was burned. It avoided all stoves ever after. Cats aren't capable of thinking in discriminate ways. Take on a philosophy of nonavoidance by seeing that all people in a certain age or sex category are not alike. If you are a female who was taken advantage of by a male try to accept the fact that not all men are alike. Ask yourself, "Was it such a bad experience that I'm willing to risk everything as far as any future associations with men?"
10. *Take your fear with you.* Fear of the unknown tends to evaporate when you contact what lies ahead. What seemed bigger than life suddenly becomes a part of life. Moving ahead in spite of your fears often reveals your concerns as figments of your imagination.
11. *Avoid pigeonhole thinking.* Because something once happened doesn't mean it is going to continue to happen. Assuming otherwise will result in you making yourself afraid to take the next step forward.
12. *Focus on the present.* There is unlikely to be a problem that is not going on right now. People disturb themselves today in the same way as yesterday, notably by overreacting and personalizing. Rehashing alleged historical roots

may prove to be interesting but not necessarily beneficial.

13. *Make the thinking-feeling connection.* Understand that although your feelings are influenced by life circumstances, your feelings are more directly determined by your thoughts. Because you mainly feel the way you think, monitor the thoughts that immediately precede your feelings and select those that help you to feel more the way you want to feel and less the way you don't.
14. *See dissatisfaction and disturbance as separate feeling states.* Affect or influence is not necessarily disturbance. When your environment or people in it frustrate you, such deprivation need not be made dramatic. By accepting the dissatisfaction as reality, emotional disruption is acknowledged but contained.
15. *Avoid the myth that dysfunctional circumstances produce dysfunctional people.* This theory doesn't hold water when one examines the multiple interactional effects between people. Many people raised in high frustration turn out to be minimally disturbed; many reared with low frustration make themselves highly disturbed. Fatalistic views do not have the real-life evidence to back them up.
16. *Disbelieve the idea that an individual "gets" or "is given" beliefs.* Humans have free will and invent their own interpretations of their unique life happenings. If these self-manufactured ideas don't build a case for emotional self-control and self-acceptance they can be uninvented.
17. *Strike out the notion that social systems disturb people.* People bring their "upset-ability" to the system and disturb themselves about the family or social context in which they live.
18. *Question the assumption that to change the individual, his or her dysfunctional circumstances must be changed.* Removing outer problems does not transform inner problems. Individuals can be pacified when their social circumstance is restructured, but their faulty way of thinking about what adversity means for them goes untouched. As a result, they remain at the mercy of their environment.
19. *Challenge the notion that changing circumstances is easier than changing individuals.* In practice, individuals

change quicker than systems and can rise above them. Changing individual attitudes can be more efficiently done than correcting transactions between people.

20. *Debate the idea that individuals are nearly totally dependent upon bonds with significant others.* Emotional and practical dependency are two different things. We depend on our social group to provide us with the practical advantages of living. We need not depend on others for help in accepting and finding value to ourself.
21. *See that what goes on inside the individual is more important than what goes on outside of him or her.* John Milton stated, "The mind is its own place, and in itself can make a Heav'n of Hell, a Hell of Heav'n." The focus of control in one's life is not the events that occur but the individual's way of looking at these happenings.
22. *Don't overemphasize change.* Take pressure off yourself for having emotional complications related to harsh experiences. Don't perfectionistically insist that you have to conquer your overreaction. Because one part of your life is out of place does not mean that all is lost. Accepting your current inability to come to terms with a part of your past deflates emotional tension.
23. *Debate the faulty idea that humans have needs that are required to ("have to") be met.* Believing the necessity of affirmations and validations makes it a foregone conclusion that given extenuating experiences you will automatically buckle under emotionally. Such rigid perspectives betray that human capability to take a stand against adversity.
24. *Disbelieve the idea that you can be scapegoated, demeaned, or rejected.* Others selecting against you cannot hurt you if you accept yourself. Nobody can scapegoat you but you. All rejection is self-inflicted. Not labeling yourself by someone's contrary treatment of you makes for comprehensive emotional rustproofing.

Some of these suggestions question conventional wisdom and may be difficult to accept. The temptation is to believe what one has been told simply because it is more convenient to do so. It may seem immediately easier to sidetrack yourself by scrutinizing historical, family-of-origin material. Such derailment may provide a degree of gratification, if not indulgence. However, this review distracts from two important factors: (a) You can't change what has already happened and you would do better to work hard at accepting its reality; and (b) because happiness is not externally caused, and because you and not circumstances or significant others in your situation are responsible for your feelings, you disturb yourself - whether it be yesterday, today, or tomorrow.

Expressing feelings of bitterness, rage, hurt, anger, guilt, and fear may temporarily help you to feel better; but learning how you create such unwanted emotions, and how to correct your distortions of thought, permits you to *get* better. As William Shakespeare stated: "There is nothing either good or bad, but thinking makes it so."

Love and Compatibility: The Elusive Siamese Twins of Eternal Bliss

Falling in love is like falling off a log when compared to the more difficult task of working yourself into happiness. Love as it is able to be blended with compatibility is often not the two-for-the-price-of-one package deal that, on paper, it appears to be. In fact, such an assumption is not worth the paper it's written on.

Partners tend to muscle themselves into believing that their glittering, tinseled assumption about this hard-to-come-by duo naturally goes without saying, only to regretfully discover that love doesn't conquer all - including incompatibility. After all, isn't it more immediately convenient to buy the theory that love and compatibility go together like hand in glove, or like two peas in a pod? Suckering oneself into believing that this mythical ideal does naturally exist provides a rush of relief that comes from thinking that effort and perspiration can be bypassed en route to achieving happiness.

This faulty notion can sustain a relationship until the realities that only ongoing association can bring set in. The reality of finding out what it's really like to closely commiserate with another human being - someone who is much different from, and almost if not equally as fallible and imperfect as you - kills the dream of never-ending harmony, mutual accommodation, and compliance. Such a heavy dose of reality is often interpreted as too much to accept.

Bridging compatibility gaps takes more than magic, automatic assumptions, or a commercialized view of what mutually satisfying relationships are made of. Relationships are *not* made in heaven, and they are composed of hard work, persistence, realism, acceptance, forgiveness, and perhaps above all - tolerance. The latter won't make for a compatible relationship in itself, but it is unlikely that you will have a satisfying relationship without it.

It's not easy to take the easy way out; if love is to survive everyday wear-and-tear, natural incompatibilities will probably require being worked on and worked out. The saying goes that genius is nine-tenths perspiration and one-tenth inspiration. So it is with relationships: Compatibility is the nine-tenths perspiration and love is the one-tenth inspiration. Further, it is likely that the longer the relationship lasts the more that same inspiration to stay and thrive together is likely to flow from the perspiration of routine maintenance. Preventing consistent togetherness from becoming the deathbed of love requires effort.

The remainder of this guide will present (a) reasons why love and compatibility are, more often than not, *not* on the same wavelength, and (b) practical suggestions for what can be done to build compatibility bridges instead of incompatibility walls in a love relationship.

REASONS WHY LOVE AND COMPATIBILITY ARE NOT IDENTICAL

1. *Individual differences.* A couple are naturally incompatible with one another in many ways, including what they think the good life is about. These differences will clash - if allowed to. One person's favorite food is frequently the other's poison. Mates have tendencies and tastes that go in different directions for no special reason. Often these innate variances are not fully unmasked until the relationship has been underway on a day-in-and-day-out basis for a long time. It may come as a surprise to many when they discover that these divergent traits, preferences, tastes, and characteristics turn out to be the

same features that attracted them to each other in the first place. Opposites may attract, but similarities are more likely to stay together.

2. *Human fallibility.* Humans bring their imperfections into a relationship only to find a partner who was looking for something better. Unless one is mated with a rare bird - an exceptionally tolerant partner - this expectation will only rub the wrong way more strongly.
3. *Human variability.* Humans are not only different from one another but also vary within themselves from one day, hour, or moment to the next. Moods are subject to change, and when such emotional transition is in a contrary direction, conflict and incompatibility are made more accessible.
4. *Human insistences.* Insisting that because you love someone, that person is duty bound to make himself or herself compatible with your wishes and values is like trying to force a round peg into a square hole. Stubbornly protesting against your partner having the gall to exercise free will and not your will is undemocratic and disruptive.
5. *Gullibility and suggestibility.* When individuals permit themselves to fall in love they do so for the better, overlooking the worms in the apple of their eye. Part of this philosophy of "They can do no wrong" is related to ideals, spoon-fed by the media, that couples allow themselves to be hustled by. Notions such as "Love is all you need" lead to a rude awakening; the blind lead the blind down a lot of blind alleys - without ever finding the way home.
6. *People change.* What you see at the beginning of a relationship is often not what you get after a few months or years. Changing people in changing times increases the likelihood of disagreements and boundary disputes. Personal development strides in a different direction from what was originally expected could be disastrous to the relationship if not managed effectively.
7. *People refuse to change.* Refusing to bend without breaking, bullheadedly or complacently maintaining the status quo, promotes a dull, mediocre relationship at best

and a conflictual, argumentative one at worst. Without efforts at compromise and collaboration, love is unlikely to be accompanied by compatibility.

8. *Emotional dependency.* Regardless of how much you love someone, if you additionally make yourself emotionally dependent on that person you will likely end up frequently throwing cold water on the relationship. Compatibility is not enhanced by making someone so vital to your existence that you convince yourself you can't get along without him or her. Loving someone for the purpose of validating your existence puts the kind of pressure on a relationship that runs counter to cultivating common ground.
9. *Outside distractions.* Compatibility goals are more easily derailed when there is an abundance of outer world dilemmas and decisions to make at the same time. You and your mate are unlikely to have the same perspective on issues of finances, in-laws, job pressures, raising children, and so on no matter how much you hope for that constant.
10. *Grandiosity.* Deflate the fantasy belief that your loving partner is an extension of your wishes, with a mind like your own. The reality is that neither the world nor your loved ones in it were made for you.
11. *Tendencies to personalize.* Taking to heart mutual differences, as reflected in your thoughts, tends to dampen love that once glowed. Thinking that "If you loved me you wouldn't have the gall to disagree with me" creates a relationship that is conditioned upon your requiring that mutual values, like mutual love, consistently overlap. "If you don't like my values you don't like me" is an equation for relationship misery that will lead to the demise of your most well-intentioned accommodating efforts.
12. *Tendencies to overreact.* Throwing kerosene on divergent views creates conflictual bonfires that can put a strain on an otherwise reasonably conducted relationship. Exaggerating the importance of two people differing amplifies the distance between love and compatibility.
13. *Perfectionism.* Believing that perfect amicability has to be the byword, and that shared arrangements are required

to be just so, comes up short when measured against the imperfections that exist between people. Such requirements for mandatory exactness drive a wedge between the ideals of love and compatibility.

If exclusive love and compatibility are not to be found as part of this world, what can be done to make it convenient for relationships to develop in this world? The following guidelines are likely to increase the options of bridging togetherness.

1. Before accepting what you believe to be true about the other's contributions to your problems (e.g., "*He makes me* upset!" "She *must* act according to my approval and *must not* act according to my disapproval"), honestly ask yourself, "Where is the evidence for my notions and ideas?" If you discover that there is no evidence, and therefore you can't prove your beliefs, change them: "I upset myself about my partner, now let me see if I can figure out how I can get myself un-upset." "He has free will and can freely choose to act the way he wants, *not* the way I want."
2. Avoid giving unsolicited, unasked-for advice.
3. Really push yourself to try harder to better understand the other rather than getting the other to understand you.
4. Be more interested in extending and accommodating the relationship than in being right.
5. Make yourself harder to resist by providing consistent attention to your partner's wishes, preferences, and desires.
6. Freely applaud your humanness by openly admitting your mistakes.
7. Openly apologize when appropriate.
8. Avoid trying to convince the other of something he or she doesn't want to be convinced of.
9. Overreact less; for instance, minimize "Isn't it awful that . . ." and "I can't stand this. . . ." Accept yourself more; for instance, "I don't have to judge myself by my relationship flaws."
10. Realize the truth of sayings such as: "The art of being wise is knowing what to overlook" and "Silence is (sometimes) golden."

11. See that it is in your best interest to make a point to focus on the appreciatory and to neglect the depreciatory traits, characteristics, and features of the other.
12. Send "I" rather than "you" messages, for instance, "I feel . . ." rather than "You make me feel. . . ."
13. Criticize very selectively, and when doing so don't criticize the person; only criticize a specific part of his or her behavior.
14. Don't tell the other what you think he or she is thinking.
15. Learn to tell your partner how you feel without telling him or her off.
16. Learn to take the responsibility for controlling your emotions by monitoring your thoughts, ideas, and statements to yourself that create your feelings.
17. Avoid once-and-for-all, black-or-white, all-or-nothing thinking, for instance, "You always," "never," "every time."
18. Avoid digging up the past and opening up old wounds.
19. Stay away from finger pointing, whose only purpose is proving who's the "good guy" and who's the "bad guy."
20. Avoid keeping score by calculating whose "turn" it is to apologize or give in, designating who is more right or more wrong, or tabulating who's contributing more to the relationship.
21. Don't attempt to mind-read. Don't assume you know what the other is thinking or feeling without asking, or expect the other to know what you're thinking or feeling without you having to tell him or her.
22. Don't hit below the belt by purposefully going to work on the other's "sore spots."
23. Put forth three little words: "I understand you." Do this by training yourself to become an active sounding board of not only what your partner says, but also the feelings behind what is being said. Using yourself as an echo of your loved one's feelings communicates not just a concern for *what* is being said, but also the *who* behind the words.
24. See and seize your relationship as an opportunity to work on your own mental health in increasing your capacity for tolerance, acceptance, grace, and forgiveness.

25. More fully accept and strongly convince yourself that although they are wrong in being wrong, people do have a right to: fail, make mistakes, err, pull boners, blunder, flaw, goof, have faults and shortcomings, or be wrong.

The belief that love and compatibility are one and the same sets in motion a chain of misunderstandings. Unless broken with a more realistic and accepting perspective such linkage will promote the kind of emotional fallout that often ends with a long-term relationship becoming the deathbed of love.

Lovc can bc sharcd. For a timc, compatibility may ccment a relationship further. However, often sooner rather than later such common ground is found to be a "flash in the pan" that is not able to stand the test of time. Enjoy it while you can - and then dig in and welcome yourself to the real world of individual differences. Be glad you and your partner do not have the same tastes and values, for if you did there would be no human uniqueness, variety, or individuals - only clones from the same model. When your partner was conceived the mold was thrown away. Try to be happy for yourself and your partner in enjoyment of these same personality divergences. It is more likely you will learn from someone who thinks differently than you. Similar views tend to lead to more of the same: a business-as-usual outlook. See your disagreements as an opportunity to expand your knowledge base rather than as a method of shrinking your development potential.

One partner asked the other: "Do you believe in love?" The other replied: "Yes, especially if the other pays half the rent." How about the advisability of believing in compatibility? Mohammed once said, "Tell me a mountain has moved and I'll believe. Tell me that a person has changed his personality and I'll believe not." The sometimes regretful but true reality is that human beings don't reorganize their personalities very much. For this reason it would be wise to be realistic when sizing up an intimate bonding attachment. When contemplating the ideal of love and compatibility - believe not. Just because your partner sometimes makes convenient the warming of the cockles of your heart, that does not imply that love and compatibility automatically go together. Making short-range allowances of understanding and acceptance while using practical means to deal with the given discrepancies will assist in saving long-range relationships.

Taking It Lying Down And Standing Up for Yourself at the Same Time: Silence Is Golden

William James stated that the art of being wise is knowing what to overlook. Truth is often unwelcome to those who like their ear tickled in the form of you saying what they want to hear. It is not always practical to express oneself openly in the face of likely disagreement. Rational behavior is to conduct yourself in line with your long-range best interests - which often means keeping your big yapper shut. The fact that a decent respect for silence often yields personal advantages frequently goes unnoticed. The theme of this guide is that although silence is not as dramatic an act as direct, assertive behavior, it is often consistent with the goals of personal and relationship satisfaction.

Staying out of the way of the consequences of an undesirable experience as best you can rather than fighting back may appear cowardly. Others' appearing to take advantage of you makes it convenient for them to label you as a patsy or a doormat. It is rarely seen that such a position can be a rational way of standing up for yourself; rather than being against your best interests, such behavior can often contribute to your long-range happiness and survival. Sayings such as "Live coward, dead hero," and "Discretion is the better part of valor" describe this type of behavior. Following are some examples:

1. In a job where your supervisor thrives on criticizing you harshly or in some other way abuses his or her authority, it may be better for you not to fight fire with fire. If asserting yourself in such circumstances is likely to result in your being fired, it would be to your practical advantage to agree with yourself to keep silent until you find a place of employment more to your liking. In such circumstances it would be helpful to ask yourself: "Do I want to feel better now by telling my boss where to go, or do I want to feel better in the future by being able to continue paying my bills?" As hard as it might be to put up with such unfair treatment, it would be even harder not to do so if it meant ending up in the unemployment lines.
2. When raising a strong-willed child it is often better, when practical, to deal with such opposition with heavy doses of enormous detachment. Care less without becoming uncaring; take a nonverbal step back rather than two verbal steps forward. These moves will save the emotional wear and tear that comes from trying to teach a child who is acting temperamentally something that he or she doesn't want to learn. Frowns, complaints, and other annoying antics can be contained by abrupt avoidance - just turning away. For example, when a child openly complains that he or she doesn't think it's fair that he or she is required to take out the garbage, complete silence will give him or her less to react against. Taking the wind out of his or her sails by this silent turning away protects you from getting caught up in his or her problems and gripes.
3. Associating with a relative who is acting difficult is no fun. A sibling or in-law who often finds criticism, backbites, or in other ways attempts to play the role of agitator can sometimes best be dealt with by leaving well enough alone. If you see that when these people throw out the bait you do not have to bite, they will likely cast less often. Little conflict remains when you let insinuations, double messages, and misinformed opinions die on the vine by not responding to them.

By not bringing the attention to yourself that would come from taking aggressive issue, you are doing well for yourself in two ways: First, the misery-likes-company mentality of your relative is not accommodated. Your neglect discourages his or her emotional free-loading activity. Bad behavior gone unnoticed is less likely to occur again. Second, by avoiding playing his or her game you are less likely to be identified as being on his or her team. Others who have received similar barbs from this person are likely to look at you in an admirable way, perhaps using your example as a future guide for their conduct toward this person.

4. When being scolded by someone in authority it will often be in your favor to say nothing. When someone has more leverage than you, simply listening in seeming agreement may be the best you can do to stand up for your long-range best interests. Contradicting what is being said may make it convenient for this individual to make himself or herself even more annoyed, resulting in even harsher consequences. If an agent of control such as a teacher or police officer is trying to drive home a point that you may disagree with, quietly go along with the drift of his or her message to protect your best interests. Allowing authority to have the last word can provide advantages when it appears there are none.
5. Living with a marital partner who is highly sensitive to disagreement is perhaps the ultimate test of patience and prudence. When, all things considered, you view your marriage as favorable in spite of your partner's irritability, overlooking such negative mannerisms might help preserve what all-in-all is a good thing. To enter into controversy without first seeing such differences as being but one part of the total relationship ecology is to risk losing what you value. Tiptoeing around rather than stomping down on your loved one's upset can be a quiet way of doing yourself a big favor.
6. When in a discussion with daily associates, objecting to matters of group agreement may not be wise. If you suspect that open confrontation may lead to the group's conspiring to avoid you in the future, and you would find such bias highly inconvenient, you'd best maintain the

cooperation of your social group. Save your assertive ideals for circumstances that will be less likely to lead to such practical disadvantage. Disagreement for the sake of disagreement will not likely be in your favor. It is silence, not controversy, that often has a life of its own, and improves life.

Making allowances for others' authority, disturbances, and advantages by cultivating a decent respect for your own silence in difficult circumstances has a number of practical personal and interpersonal advantages. These include:

1. *Builds tolerance confidence.* Tolerance in itself won't make for a happier life, but it is unlikely that you will have a delightful existence without this disciplined trait. Many things in life that you want you may not be able to achieve. Demonstrating to yourself your ability to put up with what you don't like allows you perspective to the discomfort that accompanies experiences that fall short of the mark.

   Increasing your emotional stamina for what you don't like can be accomplished by telling yourself statements like the following: "I might feel better if I say what's on my mind in the short run, but I sure won't be better off in the long run; it would be best if I do what is better for me over the long haul." "I don't have to take what she is saying personally; her statements reflect her opinion - and her opinion doesn't equal me." "Keeping still doesn't make me a weakling - in fact, it is a component of strength because it keeps me out of trouble with my social group." "In this situation, putting myself at odds with those who have authority over me is definitely *not* doing myself a favor - I'll instead *do* myself a favor by attentively listening to what they have to say without provoking them further." "What is being said here is not the end of the world, and though I certainly don't like the content, I can stand what I don't like." "There are two things I can always do in this or any other situation in my life: tolerate something and accept myself. Let me see how I can use this tough situation to practice these two ever-present options!" Such statements to yourself allow you to lead with thoughts that can provide the power to bear with and possibly eventually influence difficult-acting people.

2. *Demonstrates love.* Muffling yourself can be a loving act when you realize that outspokenness will likely assist in fueling the emotional fires of a sensitive-acting peer. Not taking people as seriously as they are taking themselves is a very caring act. The less you make out of other people's upset the sooner they are likely to wind down their disenchantment. Allowing people to make themselves upset without your hassling them goes a long way toward not blowing such disgruntlement out of proportion.
3. *Expresses confidence in the other.* The communication about the silent communication is "I don't think you're an emotional cripple, and I think you can handle your concerns on your own, so I'm not going to rush in and take care of you or in any way try to do your work for you by trying to make you happy." Such a vote of confidence conveys your belief in the other's ability to assume responsibility for his or her own feelings.
4. *Invites respect.* Upon analysis, silent restraint is likely to be viewed as a model for inner strength. Your adversaries may interpret your unexpected unresponsiveness as a sign of inner fortitude. When people openly express their upset toward you they often expect a counterattack or a defensive posture. Not giving in to such measures of disturbance may come as quite a surprise to the contrary-acting other who expects a return in kind. Getting his or her attention by your inattention to his or her upset may leave him or her in awe of your absence of overreaction.
5. *Builds upon preexisting unconditional self-acceptance.* It takes a secure person, someone who is well grounded in a foundation of self-acceptance, to overreact less and accept himself or herself more in the face of criticism or disagreement. Silent restraint can help to cement a view of self that permits this for no special reason, without any external props acceptance.
6. *Promotes undamning acceptance of others.* When applied properly, quietude neutralizes vengeance and enlists compassion and forgiveness. Nonjudgmental restraint - where you acknowledge your dislike for others'

messages but accept them and their right to expression even when it is against you - will generate the type of tolerance that will be helpful in living in a world that is often more prickly than desired. Understanding that although you think your adversary's views are bad, you accept that he or she is not bad for having them, is the key to this noncondemning philosophy.

7. *Can improve future relationships.* If one of the best ways to win people over is to accept them the way they are, then taking a verbal step back rather than two confrontational steps forward would seem to be preferable. Acceptance is a rare commodity, and by quietly demonstrating acceptance you encourage your associates to gravitate more toward you.
8. *Reduces aggressive conflicts.* A "good" fight does not clear the air - it pollutes it. It takes two things to make a fight: an issue to fight about and two people who are willing to throw gasoline on that issue. By choosing to not be a part of the action you minimize harmful fallout from verbally aggressive encounters.
9. *Encourages the other to look within.* When other people are left to shadow box with themselves, they are encouraged to interpret what their antics tell them about their way of doing business with the world. Their exaggerated reaction highlights their insecurity, leading to greater likelihood that they and others will evaluate how their emotional drama, rather than your alleged wrongdoing, is the more important issue.

This does not mean that there is no room for assertive activity, but such forwardness is best saved for select occasions, when it can be seen as helping to gain more long-range pleasure than pain. Behaviors are often selected because they satisfy an immediate whim rather than because they support long-range goals. If, after calculating the pros and cons, you decide that standing up for yourself by openly expressing yourself is likely to be to your advantage, by all means do so!

On the other hand, if after weighing the odds of instant pleasure against pain down the road, you gather that there is likely to be more of the latter and less of the former, stand up for yourself by taking the matter lying down. You do have rights of free expression, but at times you would do better to not exercise those rights; this is especially true if you believe that you also have a responsibility to yourself not to die with your rights on.

I'm Not OK - You're Not, Not OK: The Rating Game and Its Contributions to Emotional Indigestion

Perhaps self-judgments aren't the root of *all* emotional evil - just most. Self-evaluation seems to be a favorite human pastime, and contributes much to defeating the search for happiness in life. A parent who passes judgment on himself or herself if his or her child doesn't turn out well in the eyes of the community; someone who puts himself or herself down for losing out in love; a worker who makes himself or herself feel inferior after being passed over for promotion; these are all representative examples of this syndrome of getting after oneself. Whenever you rate yourself your emotional health is up for grabs.

Giving yourself a good review is likely to lead to giving yourself negative appraisal eventually. People tend to value themselves for *special reasons* (i.e., "I'm OK, I have high self-esteem, my self-concept is high, I have much self-worth - because I'm doing many of the right things"). Thinking that you're "good" because of your successful performances is likely - probably sooner rather than later - to be reversed into thinking you're "bad" when you fail. Playing this rating game, with its self-assessment flip-flopping, accounts for many of the mood swings people give themselves.

Rational-emotive therapy (RET), as invented by Dr. Albert Ellis over 35 years ago, actively tries to abolish what other methods try to promote. RET takes notable exception to the notions (a) that humans can prove their worth and (b) that such attempts at proclaimed self-worth are of benefit to their happiness. RET does encourage you to judge your actions and to hold yourself responsible for these outcomes, but not in a way that encourages you to get up on yourself for your advantages and down on yourself because of your disadvantages. If you didn't give yourself an honest appraisal of your deeds and traits you would not be motivated to correct your mistakes. If you evaluate your behaviors and take your evaluations on further and judge yourself along with your actions, the emotional effect will be like a yo-yo.

Self-rating is a wolf in sheep's clothing; this may be a difficult idea to swallow, but it is likely to strengthen your stomach on the way down. Controlling for success - claiming that you have more self-worth or higher self-esteem because of your successful projects or others' approval - is a temporary band-aid in dealing with the realities of ongoing human imperfection. A more permanent, major surgery solution that provides more comprehensive emotional rustproofing would be to take on ideas that permit you to accept yourself regardless of the fruits of your labor or others' appraisals.

Going mainly for practical solutions to problems of human existence is very tempting. It may seem more convenient to quickly replace a loved one who abandoned you than to emotionally establish yourself as an enjoying person in your own right *before* you seek a replacement. It may appear easier to immediately prove yourself through your ability to succeed rather than accepting yourself with your failures first. Such quick decisions at best may temporarily help you to *feel* better; but they are unlikely to allow you to *get* better. Your self-judgmental belief system remains unchecked, leaving your emotional well-being subject to your ability to cut muster. You will unlikely be able to more fully accept yourself using these methods. Gaining a fish (achieving success, gaining love and approval) will allow you to eat for today; learning how to fish (accepting yourself without those conditions attached) will enable you to eat for the rest of your life.

Understand that you are different from your behavior. Humans are too complex and ever-changing to judge as "worthwhile," "less worthwhile," or "worthless" by the many both good and bad things that they do. Recognizing this affords the following advantages:

1. *Lets you be yourself without proving yourself.* Knowing you're not on stage and don't require a good review from your critics permits you to be more at ease with your social group. Such affordable informality is likely to make you more fun to be around. Increased harmony and social opportunity will likely follow.
2. *Encourages personality experimentation and well-roundedness.* Understanding that you're not at risk as a human being and that you're not a failure for failing has its advantages. When success is not your lifeline you will try to succeed more often - in a clearheaded way. Consequently you will likely explore dimensions to your capacity to experience life that you didn't know existed.
3. *Increases compassion toward others.* Compassion and forgiveness start with your attitudes toward yourself. Not giving yourself a report card with a bad mark makes convenient the same permissive views toward others' ever-present flaws. By getting rid of self and other judgments, tolerance levels in the form of your ability to better put up with what you don't like are increased.
4. *Increases openmindedness.* If you rate others you will likely create anger if it is a negative rating and intimidation if the numbers are favorable. If you pass judgment on yourself you will make yourself depressed or guilty if it is a negative rating and anxious if it is a positive score. The latter occurs because you are likely to worry about keeping up the count if you believe your value to yourself depends on it. All of these ratings are the same emotional choice-blocking hearse with different license plates. Flip-flopping ego messages mean pigeonholed thinking, which makes it hard to be clearheaded. Flexible outlooks result when judgments of self and others are put to rest.
5. *Curtails approval seeking.* Taking on the belief that others' opinion of you does not equal you takes much pres-

sure off your relationship with them. Knowing that you will not emotionally melt when confronted with another's disapproval makes for accessible, refreshing dialogue that is open and above board.

6. *Abandons achievement needs.* Understanding that accomplishments are nice but not necessary allows you to focus more on enjoying what you're doing rather than proving yourself by your projects. Realizing that you're not a better person because of your achievements makes it easier for you to enjoy the ways you are better off because of them.
7. *Sidesteps the misery equation.* Thinking that your deficiencies are the same as you is an accounting system that hampers effective living. When you think that your personal well-being depends on your efficiencies you will put yourself one down in the face of your deficiencies. Worry results from the notion that you cannot fail, lest you become your failures.
8. *Destroys the ego.* With nothing to prove about yourself there is no basis for self-blame. Understanding that you're not on trial permits you to treat yourself to a trial period of no self-downing. You continue to get after your behaviors but you cease to get after yourself. As a result, you accomplish more and condemn less.
9. *Minimizes hurt and anger.* Self-depreciation precedes hurt. If you don't put yourself down for not being able to control for the success you would like, it is unlikely you would feel hurt. Blaming yourself for not getting someone else to not dislike you will also bring on the helpless emotion of hurt. Depreciation of others in the form of "You made me feel hurtful - you no-goodnik!" allows anger to make its not-so-grand entrance. By avoiding self-judgments you can nip such excess emotional baggage in the bud.
10. *Encourages moral behavior.* To act immorally is to hurt a human being - and that includes yourself. When you whip yourself with your shortcomings you do much harm to yourself. By giving up such self-condemning behavior you become a human being who acts more morally.
11. *Hits the emotional disturbance nail on the head.* Most difficulties of the world boil down to ego, self-proving

problems. If humans would cut down on their tendencies for self-evaluation there would be little basis for emotional anguish. Knowing that you are not dependent on others' cooperation or approval and your performances or achievements to accept yourself takes away the foundation of anger, anxiety, guilt, and depression. Not measuring yourself in accordance with outside forces allows you to unshackle yourself from the self-assessment ties that bind you up emotionally.

Consider the following suggestions for avoiding the self-measurement trap:

1. *Judge behaviors and traits, not people.* Avoid overgeneralizing from what you do to who you are. See that you do certain things, but you are not what you do. By not defining yourself by your outcomes you will take much pressure off yourself and your relationships with others.
2. *Appreciate human variability.* See that humans are infinitely different from one another, and also different within themselves from one moment to the next. Don't buy into the common assumption that if you differ you are bad.
3. *Accept human fallibility.* Understanding *and* convincing yourself that humans have a right to do what they naturally do - be wrong - discourages people rating. To think that humans don't have a right to be wrong is to believe that they don't have a right to be human. To err is human; to blame and judge, unfortunately, is even more human.
4. *Appreciate human complexity.* Humans are made up of a large number of traits. Any one or several of those things about them does not measure the total person. It's silly and self-defeating to itemize and tabulate your strengths, accomplishments, and approvals from others and conclude that they increase your self-esteem, self-worth, or heighten your self-concept. Such listings will come back to haunt you in that if you esteem or judge yourself as good due to the favorable side of the ledger, you will likely put yourself down for the negative portion of your self-itemization.

5. *Don't overextend your disadvantages.* Because you are currently at a bad station in life, don't give yourself a double whammy by putting yourself down besides.
6. *Don't inflate others' opinions.* See that when others think badly of you, it is a reflection of their views, not a mirror of yourself.
7. *Rivet rational self-talk.* Practice giving yourself self-accepting messages until it becomes the natural way for you to think. Practice daily forceful self-statements such as "Lighten up," "Go easy," "Give yourself some slack," "Be more permissive with yourself," "Don't pass judgment on yourself," "Condemn the sin but not the sinner," "I sometimes do stupid things - but I'm not stupid," and "I'm not a louse when I act lousily."

Self-judgments hinder the goal of personal happiness because they will have you crying at yourself more often than laughing. If your goal is to do more laughing than crying, don't buy into a commercialized view of self-image. Be yourself rather than trying to impress others. Try to do well for reasons of practical advantage rather than to prove yourself. Don't lust after what others define as ingredients for self-esteem, but define for yourself the way you choose to look at yourself. Try to see that the one thing you can practically always do is accept yourself. No special reasons are required. By seeing that you're neither OK nor not OK you will likely make your life OK - if not better!

Exposing the Tarnish on the Sacred Cows of Parenting

Parenting is often oversimplified. As a group, parents take themselves too seriously and the effects of their parenting too literally. They look for and are told recipes and are given assurances where there are none.

Not realizing that the world doesn't run in orderly cycles, parents lead themselves to believe that if they do many of the right things in child rearing (e.g., provide heavy doses of tender loving care), they can expect to raise children who are relatively emotionally healthy. On the other hand, parents believe that if they do many of the wrong things (e.g., are unduly harsh with or critical of their children), they are likely to produce children who have emotional problems.

Assumptions such as these are not valid and point perhaps to the only golden rule of parenting: There is no golden rule. When scrutinized for outcome, many of the classic, standard operating procedures for raising children can be seen to have loopholes. What they are and why they often backfire, have limitations, are not all they are cracked up to be, and are not *the* answer to everything (or anything) will be reviewed in this guide.

My objectives are (a) to encourage a sense of realism and humility for what the best parental intentions and methods can and cannot do to and for children, and (b) to invite acceptance of the uncertainties of parenting and consequently of oneself. To acknowledge that nothing is foolproof is to invite that breath of fresh air that accompanies acceptance of uncertainty.

The following four sacred cows of parent-child relationship building, though "American as apple pie," are oversold. Consequently, when parents follow these cultural prescriptions and still have child-rearing complications, they are likely to make themselves feel disillusioned, powerless, and down on themselves for not being able to make these "sure-fire" methods work for them.

I hope that the following different ways of looking at alleged tried-and-true notions will free parents up to time test what might be best for them while opting for perhaps the highest level solution to their problems - that sometimes the solution to a parent-child relationship problem is to accept the reality that there is no immediate solution. What parents can often use more than how to make things right in their relationship with their children is to get themselves less upset when things go wrong.

MODELING

Modeling as a means of childhood learning is grossly overestimated. If modeling were a deciding factor in personality outcome children would be clones of their parents. Children do look at their parents and follow the parents' behavior patterns - sometimes; but children are choosy in what traits they take on from their parents. Children select toward patterning those characteristics of their parents that are more immediately convenient for them to model. Humans have a natural affinity toward comfort, and they actively encourage themselves to gravitate toward what seems the easier thing to do. Children select to mirror those features of their parents' behavior that are in line with their natural tendencies.

Because children are born fallible, they have preexisting tendencies toward problems. They are accidents waiting to happen. They use their parents as a convenient excuse to give vent to what already exists. For instance, a boy who excuses his actions with "I have a temper because I learned it from my father," or "I smoke cigarettes because my parents do," is failing to consider that there are a lot of ways he's not like his parents. This is so simply because he by nature leans toward being short-fused and nicotine addicted. Children who are raised by adoptive parents often will take on the eating habits of their natural parents whom they have never met. So too, this child is likely to have problems of temper control and addiction even if he had been raised by parents who were easy-going and did not use cigarettes. Also, children raised with similar models in the same family often turn out differently because they end up using their unique tendencies as a convenience item.

In fact, being too "good" a role model can backfire on parents. This is because children who see themselves as not being capable of living up to such a high-level role model may look down on themselves for not measuring up to such an exalted ideal. The implication for parenting comes from the value of accepting that even though as a parent you may seem at times to be "damned if you do and damned if you don't," you don't have to put yourself down while continuing to try to do well without perfectionistically insisting on doing the best.

PRAISE

Positive reinforcement is another parenting method that is glorified to the hilt. "Praise until you're blue in the face and everything will turn out fine" is what parents are often told. Limitations of and fallout from this sacred ideal include:

1. *Can contribute to increased dependency.* When children look for praise to document their efforts or to gain a liking of themselves they often turn themselves into bottomless pits. Once a dire need for praise is established, the issue becomes "How much is enough?" Praising a child may temporarily help him or her to feel better, but it won't get him or her past the negative self-judgments or the tendency to avoid responsibility without it.
2. *Makes convenient overgeneralized thinking.* When praised for things that they do well humans tend to jump to the false conclusion that because of their better action

they are a better person. Even when parents wisely make it a point to praise their child's "good" behavior rather than praise their child as being a "good" boy or girl, their offspring will likely take on a "now I'm a good person" self-judgment.

This is not to say that praise does not have its advantages; it's pleasant to give and receive praise, and it can be encouraging and helpful toward motivation. However, these merits are better gained by giving praise now and then rather than continuously. It's best not to expect such affirmations to produce miraculous results in your child's development.

3. *Often misinterpreted.* Especially if provided too enthusiastically, praise is often interpreted as meaning you expect perfect performance in the future. When children expect perfection from themselves, or think you expect it from them, they will likely find many excuses to not follow through with expectations.
4. *Disguises ulterior motives of the sender.* Praise often has a deceitful, manipulative component to it. It frequently is given because we want someone else to do something that will make life easier for us in some way. At other times it is provided to convenience the receiver to think well of himself or herself. The message "Feel good about yourself because of the good things I say about you" invites the receiver to be beholding to you. After all, if you are feeling good about yourself in direct proportion to the praise I deliver, you will likely feel bad about yourself when I don't deliver such sparkling provisions. Children are unknowingly encouraged to pass judgment on themselves by whether or not they are praised by significant others. If they are to have "high self-esteem" when favorably acknowledged, then they acquire "low self-esteem" when unfavorably recognized.
5. *Can contribute to a "spoiling effect."* Some children look for their main source of reinforcement within themselves. They find intrinsic value in a job well done. Such children thrive less favorably when they receive something they don't need and which they are capable of providing for themselves. Some even discourage or resent unsolic-

ited acknowledgement. Praise is a two-way street. Its efforts depend on the sender and how he or she honestly intends it, and also on the receiver and how he or she interprets it. Some children are more reinforceable than others and interpret affirmative messages differently. Praise may end up being important for some children some of the time, but it's best not viewed as an all-important part of parenting strategy.

TENDER LOVING CARE (TLC)

TLC is one of the most frequent suggestions that come under the heading of "a child can't get enough." This sacred cow of parenting has three limitations. First, parental efforts to make the love connection with their children many times don't get through. Children are by nature limited in their capacity to absorb love. Many others are too absorbed in navigating their own development to appreciate their parents' love.

Second, although open demonstration of parental love may temporarily perfume children's tendencies to get down on themselves, it won't get at their basic problem of not being better able to fully accept themselves. They go from "I'm a bad person because I can't get important people in my life to love and accept me" to "Now that I'm loved and approved of by those important people, I'm a somebody." Such a belief system won't get them by their mistaken notion that they are nobody until somebody loves them.

Third, children will often use their parents' love as a bargaining chip, or a lever of parental control. When a parent puts excessive emphasis on repeatedly and strongly telling the child "I *really* love you" - with an undercurrent of dependency - the child is likely to use such overkill against the parent. Children frequently withhold acknowledgement of their parents' love if it will get them something better. For parents to communicate to their child "I love you so much, and when you won't accept my love I'm miserable" invites trouble. Children will milk such parental dependency for all it's worth in the form of gaining more advantages for themselves. Try to communicate your love for your child to him or her, but don't make yourself dependent on being heard.

COMMUNICATION

What the communication experts fail to tell you is that many times when people learn how to communicate better, their relationship gets worse! Open discussions are fine and dandy, but only against a background of tolerant listening. When parents and children start to talk more they often say things the other doesn't want to hear. Unless they learn to move away from the notion of "Everyone is entitled to my opinion," their discussions are likely to lead to even more arguing and resentment. Try to communicate with your child, but don't deify such efforts. Lead with your positions. It's silly to talk with your child as if you don't have values, but remember, it's equally naïve to expect your child to agree with and take on your values.

If no parenting method is foolproof, where does this leave a parent? Beyond positive modeling, praise, TLC, and communication is reality - for better or for worse; accepting this can go a long way toward reducing parental pressures. Taking on a way of thinking that allows you to do well in this time-limited responsibility of parenting, without thinking you have to do the best or better than anyone else, can help to promote clearheadedness. Once parents are established in an attitude that is more permissive, accepting of uncertainty, and self-accepting, they can better choose those methods that will allow them to get more parenting mileage more often - while accepting those deficiencies that remain.

A review of the four sacred cows of parenting, including the mistaken notions behind each and the countering premises, can be found on pages 131 to 133.

PARENTAL SACRED COWS DISPUTED

SACRED COW	MISTAKEN ASSUMPTIONS	COUNTERING, CORRECTED PREMISES
1. Modeling	"The apple doesn't fall too far from the tree; children learn what they see."	"If children learned only what they saw in their parents, they would become clones of their parents. This is far from the truth."
	"Because children learn what they see, if they have problems either now or later in life, they got it from the people they see the most - their parents."	"Children are selective about what they copy in their parents or in anyone else."
	"Parents should always be a good example to their children because if they aren't, children will automatically follow their bad example. Thus, parents are an all-powerful determiner of their child's personality."	"Children, like all humans, are born remarkably imperfect and therefore have preexisting tendencies toward problems."
2. Praise	"Children require praise if they are to be motivated in life."	"Praise in some ways is nice, but certainly not necessary. In fact, some children's main source of reinforcement is themselves."
	"Positive reinforcement can do nothing but good, and such foolproof efforts should be heaped on children day and night."	"Sometimes children make themselves into bottomless pits of praise and dependency by looking for praise before they can motivate themselves or accept themselves."

SACRED COW	MISTAKEN ASSUMPTIONS	COUNTERING, CORRECTED PREMISES
2. Praise *(Cont'd)*	"You can never praise too much."	"Often, children will think they are a good person when you praise them and a bad person if you forget to."
		"When looked at honestly, praise is frequently intended to be more for the benefit of the sender than the receiver, that is, so the receiver will be encouraged to convenience the sender in some way."
3. Tender Loving Care (TLC)	"Children require consistent love if they are to be anything but sad sacks as adults."	"Love can be a very nice thing, but if it is necessary, how do some children survive and in some cases thrive without it?"
	"All children are capable of benefiting greatly from open displays of love and affection, and therefore, parents should regularly show their tender feelings toward their child."	"Children, like all people, are limited in everything they do - including their capacity to give and receive love."
	"Because openly loving one's child is sacred, parents cannot put too much emphasis on this all-important ingredient."	"In truth, many, perhaps most, children are too hung up on themselves to give and/or receive love. Furthermore, more than a few of these same children will often use their parents' enthusiasm for loving them against the parents.

3. Tender Loving Care (TLC) *(Cont'd)*		For example, if parents communicate that 'I love you so much that when you won't accept and return my love, I'm miserable,' the child may purposefully respond limply to his or her parents' affection in an effort to control them. If children think well of themselves (judge themselves to be good) simply because their parents love them, they are likely to never get around to *fully* accepting themselves.
4. Communication	"Communication is the answer to everything when it comes to solving problems of human relationships generally and parent-child relationships specifically."	"Communication, like many things, can prove helpful for some problems some of the time. However, often it is what is *not* said that proves most helpful in relationship improvement."
	"Not only is communication a necessity, but there are precise methods and techniques of communication that must be employed if communication is to prove successful."	"Groups of individuals may often have unique tactics of relating that may not go by the book but may be helpful for them."
	"Everything has to be out in the open - at all costs - if parents and children are to get along better."	"Too much of practically any good thing - including communication - can prove harmful. This is especially so when participants aren't *first* trained in the value of tolerance, that is, not upsetting themselves when their associate communicates what they didn't want to hear!"

Cutting the Umbilical Cord For the Right Reasons Rather Than Ripping It for the Wrong Reasons: Avoiding Making Yourself Dependent On Being Independent

A client of mine who is a 60-year-old housewife explained to me her position statement regarding her marriage to her husband who sometimes acted as if he takes her for granted: "You know, dear, I don't have to cook the meals, I don't have to clean the house, I don't have to do the laundry - I choose to." From her philosophy, I began to reconsider the meaning of individualism and independence and how one goes about establishing them in a purer form. I concluded that:

1. Although this woman, who did not work out of the home in her 40 years of marriage, did not have the outward appearance of emancipation, she was perhaps one of the most liberated individuals I have met.
2. Emotional independence goes far beyond acts of assertion or other purposeful behaviors that might appear symbolic of emotional self-reliance.
3. Authentic self-sufficiency begins and ends from the shoulders up. Emotional freedom is philosophically based - it comes less from your way of acting than from

your way of thinking. A prisoner in a concentration camp has the ability to establish self-reliance in a way that his or her captors might never attain.

4. It was obvious to me that this person found much delight in her self-styled independent accomplishments. Others in similar circumstances often spoil the heightened feelings of well-being that accompany efforts at self-sufficiency. By deifying an image that one believes is required to be portrayed, much enjoyment is lost in the sea of compulsive, self-proving activity.
5. Overdone displays of alleged independence are often a cover-up for feelings of insecurity, fear, and anger that are part of what is really a dependent nature. That dramatic, fist-pounding, card-burning frenzy is really a futile attempt to give vent to unwanted self-doubts.
6. People are unlikely to have an urge to take part in such confrontive behavioral disclaimers that give the appearance of independence if they *are* independent.

Examples of people who present their case for liberation in a fire-like, disinhibited, and aggressive manner are: employees who mandate themselves to work around the rules of their employer to demonstrate their free will; a marital partner who deems it essential to call his or her own shots in an effort to display seeming independence; a nagging dissenter who insists on proclaiming disapproval of what the rest of his or her social group is doing; and an adult who breaks away from his or her parent in an angry, emotional outburst to prove that he or she is independent.

All these behaviors have two common ingredients: (a) They are designed to compensate for self-deficiencies. What may appear to be a show of strength and opposition is really a mask for felt weakness and inadequacy; and (b) they are self-defeating in that the purpose that they are designed for is not accomplished. Behaviors change, but attitudes go untouched; form is achieved to the neglect of substance.

Just as diarrhea is not a cure for constipation, extremism and fanaticism are not cures for avoidance and timidity. Before explaining the difference between right and wrong reasons for the establishment of values that strive for independence, let's examine the characteristics of those who make it a dramatic point to rip away rather than deliberately move away from varying life stations. The educator Sidney Harris once said that people could use three lives: one to make a mistake, another to make the opposite mistake, and the third to reach a rational balance. Unless you are a firm believer in reincarnation, it would be best for you to avoid the following overdone and underdone characteristics of those who futilely try to accomplish liberated ends:

1. *Abruptness.* Showy attempts to emancipate oneself do not result in well-thought-out actions. Acting as if their only mandate for living is to prove their independence, their efforts are hurried and unthinking as they lead with their bias of supposed self-sufficiency.
2. *Frenzy and fanaticism.* The seeker for independence at all costs exhibits traits of overkill and overdoneness. "One way," and "the only way," become the bywords of this person, striving for the ultimate, who is acting as if driven. Heightened emotionalism follows from this limited position.
3. *Exclusiveness.* Well-roundedness is lost when extremism dominates. Life becomes focused on proving oneself in a limited way, rather than being oneself in a fuller way. Much of the extremist's time becomes consumed with his or her overriding purpose to the neglect of other life tasks.
4. *Loss of control.* When one escalates concern about one's individuality until one is emotionally consumed by it, what results is the cause irrationally running the person rather than the person sensibly directing his or her cause.
5. *Social isolation.* Immersion in the all-or-nothing project of establishing autonomy may lead to separation from one's social group. It isn't much fun to be around someone who constantly bends his or her associates' ears like a broken record. Eventually relationships are lost.
6. *Putting others down.* Others who inconvenience the independent striver's wants and purposes are condemned because they choose not to contribute to the cause of fairness and justice as he or she sees it. The philosophy of the independent-acting person is: "Everybody is entitled to my opinion; anyone who doesn't adhere to it is to

be looked down on as a second-class, less noble citizen than I."

7. *Heightened sensitivity and annoyability.* Perhaps the primary characteristic of the fixed independent seeker is his or her prickly response to practically anything or anyone that smacks of being at odds with his or her desires. The rationale is that one can't afford to do what others want or agree with them because one might lose one's treasured self-sufficiency. His or her insecurity makes it convenient to make faulty inferences about people purposefully trying to take away the striver's free will by obstructing him or her in any way.
8. *Defensiveness and overexplaining.* Making themselves dependent on their own independence, insistent strivers then make themselves compelled to provide others with a laundry list of reasons why they are the only people in the universe who have to be allowed to do what they want, when they want to. Such tedious efforts are a weak attempt to conceal their own emotionally dependent nature.
9. *Self-blame.* Because we live in an interdependent world, none of us is an island unto ourself. In an effort to perfectionistically prove their ultimate point, ultra-independent seekers set themselves up to fail. Believing that they "have to" define their autonomous territory, they are likely to put themselves down when the reality of give and take becomes obvious. Their philosophy of "50-50" - meaning others give 50 and they [independent seekers] take 50 - backs up on them.
10. *Counterattacking.* Those who actually do thwart the striver are seen as enemies to be aggressively reckoned with. By fighting fire with fire, the counterattacker takes on the same values as he or she is attacking.
11. *Denial.* In their enthusiasm for establishing their independent "space," they develop many blind spots. They are unable to get past their vehemence to see the truth to others' points of view. They cannot see that (a) most people have better things to do than being out to do them in, and (b) a certain amount of reliance on others can pleasantly lubricate social exchange.

12. *Failing to distinguish single-mindedness from narrow-mindedness.* Single-mindedness of goal while considering varying options and alternatives is one thing; the same goal with only one pure way to achieve it is another. Fixed-mindedness comes from making an objective sacred and blocking other possibilities.

The primary distinction between right and wrong reasons for seeking independence is the attitude by which you stalk this goal. Gaining and maintaining emotional emancipation is a matter of choice rather than demand. This objective is best pursued from the way of thinking that reflects your *wanting to* rather than *having to* accomplish this end. Necessitizing your goal becomes a burden; the cure then becomes the disease. Putting undue pressure on yourself to prove your independence, rather than simply being independent, is an emotional hardship. If you unshackle yourself from the strain of compulsive independent striving, you will be less at odds with your social group and more at peace with yourself.

The following ways of thinking attempt to gain independence in a pressured, nagging, self-proving way:

- "I've *got to* forcefully show others how perfectly independent I am, or they might think less of me, and that would be terrible."
- "I *have to* assert my independence, because if I don't I'll appear as a weakling, and I couldn't stand that."
- "I *need* others to recognize and acknowledge my individuality, so therefore I've *got to* openly demonstrate it to them."
- "My independence equals me. Therefore to not lose myself I *have to* at least appear boldly self-sufficient."
- "After I put my autonomous nature on display others *have to* acknowledge and respect it; if they don't they are numskulls and deserve to be subject to my despisement."
- "If I don't strongly and aggressively lead with my independent right as I *must*, others will take advantage of me and eventually do me in."
- "I have a right to be independent, and I *must* exercise that right every chance I get."

- "Independence is a good thing, and therefore I *need* to define mine regardless of the situation."
- "Others, especially those who know me best, *should* make themselves aware of, and greatly appreciate, my noble, self-reliant nature."
- "Others *should not* stand in the way of my independent strivings; when they do I will deservedly bulldoze over them."
- "My (manhood/womanhood) is at stake here so in order to not lose my (masculinity/femininity) I *must* energize myself to prove my independent point."

These futile philosophical efforts are rooted in insecurity and self-doubt rather than self-acceptance. They can be contrasted with the following more deliberate statements to oneself that promote the same self-reliant goals but for more clearheaded reasons:

- "I like, if not much appreciate, it when others treat me as a person who has a mind of his own. However, because I think that such acknowledgement would be great does not mean that others are required to provide it."
- "It's true that if I do not appear sternly independent at all times, in all places, with all people, others might deem me to be weak and inferior. However, that would be merely their definition, and I'd best not trap myself by it."
- "My independence or lack of same is simply one of many traits that I have. I'd best not stand myself in judgment by any one of them."
- "It would be better for me to not put undue pressure on myself to forever and always proclaim my independence just because I have a right to do so. I have choices, and I'd best exercise my independent option only when it's to my advantage to do so."
- "Others have a right to their own independence which at times will get in the way of my seekings. This does not mean that I would find it helpful or desirable to hold them in contempt of my not-so-sacred wishes or that I would have to act unforgiving or vindictive toward them because of their trespasses."

- "Independence is a fine goal, but like anything else it comes in various sizes, shapes, and shades of gray. I need not harp on achieving independent ends or bust a gut to prove my supposed superhuman point on the matter."
- "I don't have to forcefully obligate myself to act independent - because I am independent."
- "My gender has nothing to do with the price of petunias or with my ability to individuate. Knowing that I've got nothing to prove affords me the option of being myself with my social group rather than proving myself to my social group."

Emotional independence is there for the taking. What it takes is the rational ability to distinguish between preference and demand; to accept and be yourself without insisting that you prove yourself; and to deliberately break away rather than desperately rip away from the rigid tie that you bind yourself with.

Inhibition, Avoidance, And Timidity As Overreaction

What appears as hesitation on the outside is often an emotional flare-up on the inside. Tiptoeing around unpleasant life circumstances is an underreactive behavior prompted by an overreactive belief system. This is important to note, because until you can identify the precise dramatic way of thinking that prompts you to pull back, you will likely overlook what will be required to make yourself less avoidant. Labeling something as underdone when it really has an overdone basis will confuse the issue.

This guide will attempt to smoke out theatrical attitudes that are concealed by lax behaviors. Once these beliefs are identified they can be challenged so as to invite more forceful, constructive action.

Holding back from making a decision, avoiding completing projects long left underdone, and shyly pulling away from social contacts are situations that have a philosophical common denominator. When the sidetracking disguise is removed, what is often discovered is an overreactive way of looking at things that promotes emotional intimidation. Lacking perspective on the difficulty of the task that lies ahead, you startle yourself emotionally and that leads to removing yourself from the situation.

This guide will review what these avoidant responses are, identify the faulty belief systems that set this avoidant conduct in motion, and show how to target more optimal ways of thinking and acting.

EXAMPLES OF AVOIDANT BEHAVIOR

- Putting off making a decision.
- Backing away from a social contact/conversation.
- Holding back from seeking a promotion or applying for a different job.
- Not asking for assistance/advice when available.
- Not giving your opinion when it would be in your best interests to do so.
- Not disciplining a significant other when appropriate (e.g., a subordinate, a child).
- Not approaching a superior with a request or idea.
- Not mentioning an accomplishment.
- Not expressing feelings of love, affection, and tenderness.
- Postponing starting a new project or researching a special interest.
- Avoid doing overdue everyday domestic or work responsibilities.
- Giving in to a repair- or salesperson you differ with.
- Seldom if ever making requests of others.
- Not questioning unreasonable responsibilities given to and requests made of you.
- Not responding to unfair criticism.
- Not giving a public presentation.
- Allowing others to do things for you that you can do for yourself.
- Unquestioningly allowing others to put you off (e.g., about giving back borrowed money, a book, etc.).

OVERREACTIVE WAYS OF THINKING THAT RESULT IN INHIBITION AND TIMIDITY

- "Making the wrong decision would be devastating. What an inferior being I would be for *both* making the wrong choice *and* then allowing myself to be overwhelmed by it."

- "If I reach out for my potential associate I might feel queasy and awkward from such a first-time effort, and I couldn't stand that. In addition, he might not respond; that too would be intolerable and also lend suspect to my value to myself."
- "If I try for that promotion and fail to get it that would be too much to bear."
- "How awful it would be if I asked for assistance only to find my request was a major inconvenience for the other."
- "How horrendous to give my opinion and discover that others rejected it."
- "I couldn't tolerate the discomfort that would go along with directly correcting my associate."
- "What a dunce I would be if I failed to succeed at a new project."
- "It's just too hard to keep up with the maintenance requirements of daily living."
- "What a nerd I would be for questioning authority and then be openly criticized for doing so."
- "I could never talk in front of a group; the anxiety would kill me."
- "What an awesome thing to think of the conflict that might arise if I ask that what is mine be returned."
- "I've had it up to here - let somebody else do my work for me."
- "I'm at the end of my rope right now so I need to stay away from any situation that could create more ripples in my life."
- "I couldn't bear feeling like a fish out of water, which is what would happen if I expressed how I really feel."
- "If I bring attention to my efforts and accomplishments others might think I'm trying to be uppity and I would feel terrible."
- "If I stand my ground others might think I'm a dunce. If I don't stand my ground I would *be* a dunce!"

RATIONAL BELIEFS THAT COUNTER THE ABOVE FAULTY NOTIONS

- "Making the wrong decision would be keenly disappointing. Not coping very well in the aftermath of my poor judgment would be even more keenly disappointing. However, neither of these flubs would be the end of the world or require me to define myself as a second-class citizen."

- "Naturally when I try something for the first time I'm going to feel some uneasiness. This is the price I pay for doing something different. I'd best accept that I'm not in this world to feel comfortable; rather I'm here to experience the world, and naturally this will include some discomfort."
- "Trying and failing may not be the greatest or even one of the best things in life. However, there can be many advantages to failing such as learning things that can be put to use later. In addition, trying can have a satisfying life of its own, and it is also habit-forming."
- "I don't particularly relish inconveniencing others, but they are under no obligation to honor my request, and they have the responsibility to tell me if they wish to not provide what I ask of them."
- "Others can only reject my opinion, they cannot reject me. Only I can do that by putting myself down in the face of their ridicule."
- "If I let others get away with dodging their responsibilities I'm not doing them or myself any favors. Such corrective oversights on my part will only contribute to further cementing their bad habits, resulting in more long-range frustration on my part and more disadvantages on theirs."
- "I'd best see that it's not too hard over the course of a lifetime to tediously work on upkeeping daily tasks. Doing such laborious tasks actually gives me more time in the long run to do more interesting things, because these maintenance activities will likely lead to me being sidetracked less often due to fewer breakdowns."
- "Whatever anxiety and nervousness I might create from public appearance would be part of life, but not bigger than life. Indeed, such discomfort would not do me in because I can stand anything as long as I'm alive (and if I die from it my benefactors will probably give me a decent burial)."
- "I can afford to go further with my life, because any setbacks that I might encounter would not have to be al-

lowed to emotionally cripple or discredit me. Two things that I can always do, regardless of circumstances, is accept myself and tolerate something."

- "I want others to think well of me, but if they don't I wouldn't melt or disintegrate. Because I know that others' deficient views of me don't make me deficient, I can be freer to express myself as I choose."
- "Striving for what I want in life will not be all 'peaches and cream,' because I may conflict with others who want the same thing or for some other reason will try to block my efforts. That will prove immensely dissatisfying, but such unpleasant conflicts cannot be avoided and can be tolerated as being within the realm, rather than beyond the bounds, of reality."

People think, feel, and act their way into a lifestyle of skirting the issue. The following suggestions are countering methods to assist in thinking, feeling, and acting your way out of this avoidant approach to life.

1. *Raise your voice about the right thing.* Sound off in explanatory fashion to yourself the countering rational ideas already reviewed. Strongly convince yourself of your capacity to overreact less and accept yourself more.
2. *Get a data base.* Test out your hypothesis that if you extend rather than inhibit your efforts, your life would meet with calamity. Scientifically prove whether the results you might experience would be "too much to take" and therefore ruin and destroy you. Don't accept your drastic hunches as facts; let the voice of experience rather than the voice of doom draw your conclusions for you.
3. *Talk to others.* Check with those who have gone through what you are thinking of putting yourself through to see what kinds of experiences you might anticipate. Revealing their varied responses might help you to broaden the scope of possibilities as to what such similar efforts might mean for you.
4. *Set deadlines and penalties.* Instead of awaiting the tomorrows that never come, decide on a due date beyond which you will penalize yourself if a more direct optional response does not arrive. For example, you can contract

with yourself to work on your lacklusterness by asking the boss for a raise by next Tuesday at 4:00 p.m. If you don't complete your commitment you would penalize yourself by cleaning out the toilets, eating a food you dislike, getting up an hour earlier the next day, or doing some other task that is more difficult than your original desirable effort.

5. *Opt for elegant, higher-level solutions.* Think of the worst fate of discomfort or failure that might befall you and come to terms with your ability to survive it. This will help you to not flood yourself with all negative possibilities.
6. *Don't put yourself down.* Agree to not condemn yourself either for your shirking response or if you flounder as you branch out from your hesitations.
7. *Don't depend on others.* Don't rely on others to make it cozy for you to go forth or to assure success following your stepping out of your cocoon. In seeing that others don't owe you cooperation you will be less likely to angrily "take your ball and bat and go home" when they don't offer their supportive presence.
8. *Tell others of your intentions.* Letting others know what assertions you intend may both encourage you further and loosen you up now that your plans are out in the open.
9. *Distinguish real from imaginary consequences.* Others can frustrate and select against you. But because they can't give you feelings nor demean you, you are home free from the possibility that they will emotionally hurt or diminish you. Only you can disturb and put yourself down by telling yourself: "How horrid is others' discrimination of me; what a wretched person I must be that I cannot get others to treat me more favorably."
10. *Don't hedge.* Don't hedge your bets against yourself by qualifying your intentions with "maybe I will," "I might," "possibly I will," or "I could do that." Being more forthright in your stated intentions will likely propel the momentum that comes from a higher motivational level.
11. *Distinguish what's what with your fears.* Are you making yourself more frightened about possible negative outcomes from your initiative? Are you startling yourself

more about unwanted discomfort that might occur? Knowing what overreactive reference you are putting yourself up against will help to determine what strategies to implement in working against the problem of priority.

12. *Don't put undo pressure on yourself.* Don't insist that it be essential for you either to get rid of the problem or to learn how to cope with it better (though you may hope to do one or both). Insisting on success in problem solving will mire you in the desperation of your efforts. If you aren't able to cut muster in one area of your life, focus on that part where you have a better track record.
13. *Foresee advantages.* Go over carefully the long-range pleasure and advantages rather than the short-range pain and disadvantages of providing yourself with a bolder approach to your personal development.
14. *Preferably overcome fear of fear first.* Paul Hauck in *Overcoming Worry and Fear* discusses how by lessening your fear of discomfort you help yourself to better tolerate any circumstance that you would be inclined to avoid due to feelings of uncertainty. Consequently, you will likely introduce yourself to a more expanded life.
15. *Massed practice.* Perhaps the best way to blunt your terrors is to repeat - and repeat some more - the activity you are fearfully avoiding.
16. *No time like the present.* The best time to correct your timid habit is as soon as possible after you are aware of it. That way the laws of learning that will establish a behavior cannot build momentum.
17. *Don't make excuses.* Excuses may help you to temporarily feel better but with them you lose further control of your world.
18. *Borrow from your strengths.* Look for times you have been able to defeat your reluctances and what you were doing to encourage yourself to do so. Borrow from these past successes and put them to good use in the present.
19. *Don't give up the ship.* Accept the fact that you may be required to go down a lot of blind alleys before you find your way home. Don't resign yourself to the self-fulfilling prophecy: "That's the way I've been, that's the way I am, and that's the way I always will be."

20. *Avoid the shot-gun approach.* Put much energy into one of your priority concerns rather than doing a little bit of a lot of things but not too much of any one thing. Chances are that overcoming your inhibitions is going to require you to harness much energy to apply to your forefront concern rather than diluting your efforts in a hit-and-miss way.
21. *Take your fears with you.* Rather than wait for your discomfort to vanish you can bring it along for the ride. In doing so not only might you develop an immunity to it but you may also discover that what you were originally mortifying yourself about was a figment of your imagination.
22. *Don't wait for the perfect time.* There is no such animal as an exact time when all things and all people will come together in a way to assure success. The result of such an impossible dream is: "I need more time to find the perfect time - and probably always will."
23. *Accept that it doesn't have to be easy.* Most things that are to our advantage don't come easy. Thrusting yourself out of the starting block away from your intimidations is no exception.
24. *Don't box yourself in.* Don't put yourself in a situation where you are "damned if you do and damned if you don't." Telling yourself how excruciating it would be if you put your best foot forward and failed, while in the next breath saying how terrible it would be if you didn't try, puts you in a real emotional bind. This no-win, double-bind view will get you nowhere fast.
25. *Distinguish between can't and won't.* In their book *I Can if I Want To,* Arnold Lazarus and Allen Fay make the distinction between "can't" and "won't." To say "I can't do it" means you're beat before you start. The logical conclusion to this illogical premise is "so why try?" "I won't do it" means you have made a decision to not do it and therefore you can just as well make a decision *to* do it. "Can't" stops you in your everlasting tracks; "won't" leaves open possibilities for change.

What appears as a half-baked response is more likely to be based on an idea that is more than well-done; toned down activities are often the result of toned up philosophies; laid-back styles are frequently related to high-pitched beliefs. In the face of discomfort or negative happenings humans tend to exaggerate, overreact, and personalize. No discomfort or outcome is so small that it can't be blown out of proportion. Avoid adding fuel to feelings or events as this leads to an avoidance of life's tasks that are best dealt with more directly. Instead, see that enlightenment and acting on your entitlements comes from the perspective that in any two extremes the truth is frequently somewhere in between. Act rather than overreact or underreact; accept yourself rather than up- or downgrade yourself. Such a balanced view allows you to maintain your emotional balance in striving toward the golden mean of daily living.

Note. From *You Can Control Your Feelings! 24 Guides to Emotional Well-Being* by Bill Borcherdt.

Tickling the Apple of Your Eye's Fancy: 30 Ways to Make Room for Diplomacy and Creative Hypocrisy

Maintaining a love relationship is a difficult task at best. Mustering the resources to work - apparently against the odds - to sustain close, quality association is nothing to sneeze at. One cornerstone of relationships that is often set aside, if not frowned upon, is learning to overlook, or even to lie. Appearing one way and believing and feeling another is often viewed as manipulative and destructive, but it can be turned into an asset. If true love never runs smooth, and if all love is true by definition of its existence, why not pull together that every little bit that might help it to run *smoother*?

Having a hidden agenda in line with the best long-range interest of the relationship is a far cry from being an evil omen. Few are willing to accept the truth without breaking stride. There is a difference between a white lie and a black truth. Further, most matters that people fight about aren't viewed as vital a short time after the conflictual dust settles. Why not avoid these relationship transactions that pollute rather than clear the air? Why not make yourself harder to resist by conducting yourself in ways that extend and accommodate your relationship rather than thwart it?

Perhaps the biggest criticism of this approach is that if you "stuff" or stockpile your thoughts, feelings, and behaviors they will back up against you. Advocates of this approach greatly overestimate the disadvantages of *nonangry* restraint. Nonexpressiveness won't kill, especially when done under an umbrella of tolerance, acceptance, and forgiveness. The directness expressed in "Let it all hang out" may end up contributing much to butchering an otherwise reasonable relationship.

A distinction can be made between rational and irrational restraint. The former diminishes disturbed emotions about something you don't like or someone you don't agree with, while the latter brings on upset. Its not *whether* you quiet yourself in your effort to patronize a relationship that determines whether such efforts are an emotional problem for you, but *what you tell yourself* while you're doing it.

Irrational restraint works against your emotional well-being in that embittered emotions are created beneath your diplomatic behaviors. For example, telling yourself "He has no right to act that way," "It's terrible, awful, horrible the way she looks at things," "I can't stand it when he disagrees with me," and "What a louse she is for not thinking like me" creates anger, hostility, and - if subscribed to long and hard enough - rage.

Rational restraint comes from a different philosophical vintage. The following statements result in feelings of acceptance, possible disappointment, or annoyance - but not bitterness: "He has a right to do it his way and though I wish he wouldn't exercise that right, I'll stop myself from trying to get him to change." "It's not much skin off my nose that she looks at matters differently than I do." "I *can* tolerate differences of opinion." "Just because I disagree with her doesn't mean (a) I have to express that disagreement, or (b) she is a lousy person because I think she has a lousy opinion." Rational restraint builds up your mental health and emotional stamina while irrational restraint reinforces intolerance and wears down emotional well-being.

Examples of rational restraint in the service of relationship maintenance and survival are:

- Pretending to agree even though you disagree on nonvital issues.

- Offering strong active understanding of your partner's feelings even when you're not sure that you do comprehend them.
- Agreeing to help in spite of not feeling like it.
- Not compelling yourself to prove your point when it was not well taken to begin with.
- Being a good sport and giving in to your partner's preferences.
- Understanding and acting upon the knowledge that keeping your mouth shut can be a high-level loving thing to do. Keep in mind appropriate sayings such as "The less said the better" and "Leave well enough alone."
- *Asking* your partner for assistance rather than telling him or her you want assistance.
- Approaching controversy by actively detecting some truth to what your partner is saying.
- Making a point to *not* offer unsolicited advice. Instead, wait for the green light before correcting the other (e.g., "Would you be willing to hear out my opinion on the matter?").
- Assertively prompting the other's opinion even when you think your own is already formed on the subject (e.g., "you" questions, such as "What do you think?").
- Openly applauding your own shortcomings as this will tend to loosen up your partner's concerns about his or her own.
- Purposefully flaunting your mate's strengths and accomplishments to others - especially when he or she is within earshot.
- Periodically openly affirming the other about routine contributions.
- Telling your partner things you have never told anyone before - and identify the message as such.
- Forthrightly admitting and openly apologizing for your part in the conflictual plot even when you don't fully agree that you had such a role (e.g., "Perhaps I could have been clearer").
- Selectively going along with the other's criticisms of a third party, even when you don't fully agree with the criticisms.

- Sharing in your partner's positive sense of anticipation about a future event, even when you aren't as enthusiastic about the upcoming happening as he or she is.
- Doing things for your partner even when not inspired to do so.
- Showing enthusiasm about past events that your associate is bubbly about, even when such a past shared experience wasn't as exciting for you as it was for him or her.
- Deliberately forcing yourself to act like you feel loving toward your partner, even when you don't.
- Strongly encouraging your partner to do things for himself or herself even though you might feel left out if he or she does.
- Laughing with your partner, even at times when you don't feel like it.
- Suggesting things to do together, even when you don't feel very interested in doing so.
- Forcing yourself to talk to your partner, even when you aren't in the mood to do so.
- Using "we," "us," and "our" in conversation whether you feel such an alliance or not.
- Asking what your partner would like to do together even when you know what you would like to do - but go along with his or her selection.
- Actively seeking out areas of agreement, even if it seems like you're squeezing the juice out of a turnip.
- Laughing at yourself, even though you may not think what you did was very funny.
- Enthusiastically accepting the other's compliment even when you think what you did wasn't such a big deal.
- When asked, agreeing to work with your partner against his or her bad habits, even if you think it's his or her full responsibility.

Show me a relationship that runs smoothly without some form of contrived maintenance, and I'll show you a relationship that is made in heaven. Just as you will attract more bees with honey than with vinegar, so too are relationships better navigated with creative agreement and understanding than with compulsive honesty, openness, and directness. Making room for these well-thought-out diplomacies "as if" you felt like doi[illegible]nay well produce your finding room in your heart for the long-term perspiration out of which ongoing relationships are inspirationally made.

Tailor Making Your Thinking: 27 Ways of Dousing Rather Than Fanning the Flames of Emotional Disturbance

Confucius said: "All reform begins with the reform of language." The premise of this guide is that emotional self-control is best begun with the internal dialogue of self-created language. The two main positions of this guide are as follows:

1. How a person describes his or her concerns to self and others largely determines how he or she feels about them. People largely feel the way they think; emotions mainly validate what one thinks about a situation. Giving circumstances surplus value creates excessive emotional baggage.
2. How one sizes up one's practical and emotional difficulties has a lot to do with one's manner and plan for approaching and solving them. Looking at something that is a part of life and estimating it to be bigger than life; viewing something as important and then proclaiming it as all-important does not contribute to emotional containment. Instead, either an overkill or an underactive approach is invited.

In short, much of what is called emotion or feeling is determined by how precisely and accurately one thinks. Unfortunately the human tendency is to invent notions and ideas that promote emotional upset. Surplus, magical, unprovable ways of thinking that greatly exaggerate the significance of things or distract from personal responsibility for creating one's emotions had best be identified, challenged, and replaced with more contained, deliberate, provable descriptions if one wishes to prioritize one's emotional well-being. Restraining tendencies to exaggerate descriptions of events and circumstances will likely be required in order for one to diminish the emotional folly that flows from unrestrictiveness in thinking.

Being precise in semantics in the service of emotional accountability is something to aim for. Similar to shooting for the bull's-eye in darts or archery, aiming for word accuracy doesn't mean you're going to hit it every time, but the fact that you try is likely to mean that you will come closer to it and hit it more often en route to fuller emotional health and freedom.

The following 27 language patterns are primary contributors to emotional plaque. "Floss" them out as a preventive means of living not happily, but *happier* ever after.

1. *Finalistic thinking.* Expressions such as the following indicate more than a slight exaggeration of the human condition: "Things *always* go wrong." "I'll *never* get over this." "*Every time* I try I fail." "The *only time* something ever went right." "*Just once* I'd like to succeed." Such thinking produces a sense of helplessness and hopelessness or utter anguished frustration that assumes "That's the way it's been, that's the way it is, and that's the way it's always going to be." Uprooting such eternal belief systems and replacing them with more moderate outlooks such as "*sometimes*," "*often*," "*frequently*," "*with some regularity*," and "*up until now*" open the door for more hopeful outcomes in the future. This more permissive, flexible, unmechanical manner of interpreting matters of concern contribute more directly to emotional health.
2. *Overgeneralized ideas.* Adding to and extending well beyond the reality of a person's actions or the facts of a given outcome prompts emotional anguish that would be

better contained with a more complacent description of the situation. Typical overgeneralizing statements include: "*Everything* went wrong." "I'm *no good* at talking with people." "*All* men (or women) are untrustworthy." "I can't do *anything* right." "I have *no* skills at all." "I failed - so therefore *I'm a failure*." "I failed to succeed - thus I *will* continue to fail." "I have not succeeded in this activity - therefore I *never* will." "I was raised to believe that way - so naturally I *will* continue to think this way for the rest of my life." "When others think badly of me - I *am* bad." These elastic ideas do either of two things: (a) They leave margin for *error* but not *correction.* Such defeatist notions wall you off from the possibility of realizing your fuller potential that comes from repetition and persistence - the twin mothers of learning; and (b) they stand you in judgment by your actions or others' opinions of you.

In either case, your value to yourself and your emotional status is at the mercy of your ability to perform perfectly or your capacity to get others to think perfectly well of you. Neither is a very solid foundation from which to increase your emotional stamina. More corralled views, such as the following statements, permit a more hopeful way of interpreting life: "I didn't do well in *this* situation - but that doesn't mean it's impossible or even improbable that I won't improve next time." "Some people, *sometimes*, are not trustworthy." "I failed - but I'm *not* a failure as a person." "Others' bad opinions of me *don't* equal me." "I believed what I was told when I was younger, but I'm not young anymore and I *don't have to* carry on those ideas."

3. *Catastrophic, overreactive thinking.* Exaggerating events in a way that stretches meaning well beyond reality creates mountains of emotions in the midst of molehills of concerns. Such dramatic, "doomsday," overemphatic words as "awful," "terrible," "horrible," "overwhelming," "awesome," and "humongous" grossly distort what you are up against in your circumstances and contribute to an emotional overreaction that blocks constructive problem solving. Chicken Little's hysterical pro-

nouncement, "The sky is falling! The sky is falling!" is an example of catastrophic thinking. Such notions can have a deadening effect on emotional restraint. More tempered and deliberate rather than desperate ideas such as "unpleasant," "difficult," "undelightful," and "bearable" are likely to provide better emotional results.

4. *Fictional notions.* Ways of thinking that insist upon fairness, justice, and deservingness are fighting a losing battle. The world does not run in orderly cycles, and to command otherwise is an exercise in futility. We get what we get and what we can, not what we want or think we deserve. Statements such as "I *demand* I get what I deserve," "That's not fair as it *has to be*," and "If it's fair for them it *must* be made fair for me too" are often not meant literally. Most people want to get what they deserve *only* when it's to their advantage to do so, and what that might be often depends on whether they are asking or giving. Fortunately, there are no such animals as fairness and deservingness.
5. *Qualifying statements.* Words that convey indecisiveness, uncertainty, and watered-down commitment encourage a brand of emotional upset that comes from avoiding the persistence required to maintain consistency in approaching life's tasks. These responsibilities left unattended contribute to a style of living full of emotional upheavals. "He who hesitates is lost" - in the sea of confusion and hesitancy. Vacillating views such as "*Maybe* I will," "*Possibly* I could," and "I *might*" block long-term happiness and survival in the way similar to the fabled donkey who stood equidistant between two haystacks and ended up starving to death because he couldn't decide which haystack to eat from.
6. *Hedging comments.* A client proclaimed in the throes of commitment making: "I'll give you a definite *maybe*." Similar fence-riding patterns of expression such as "I *guess* I will," "I'm *pretty sure* I'll be there," "I *probably* will," and "I will *except* maybe I might not" promote unreliability that encourages disruptive frustration and misunderstanding between people. Associating with people who are predictable in their unpredictability in being able to depend upon them is a displeasing experience at best.

7. *Underreactive ways of thinking.* Taking a casual, flippant, "what's the difference" attitude leads to an uncaring approach to what one values in life. This attitude is reflected in statements such as: "Who cares?" "It doesn't matter anyway." "It makes no difference." "I couldn't care less." These expressions (a) minimize the meaning and vital absorption that you could otherwise experience by more fully acknowledging and affirming your values, and (b) often disguise a more dramatic, alarmist view (i.e., "I really think this matter is bigger than life so I'll camouflage my discomfort by acting the opposite and fooling myself into thinking that it is in no way even a part of my life"). These avoidance patterns prevent you from experiencing the happiness and joy that stem from coming to grips with prioritizing what you especially appreciate in life.
8. *Wonderfulizing ideas.* Positive thinking is all right - up to a point. Believing that everything is going to turn out all right just because you think so leaves you ill-prepared for the reality hassles that occur when matters don't go your way. Taking a "Pollyanna" attitude toward your experiences doesn't prepare you for rolling with life's punches. Thinking in which you like what you have and don't like or put out of mind what you don't and can't have allows for only a limited view of the human experience. "*Everything* is super, wonderful, neat," "*Nothing* is wrong," "I like things *exactly* as they are," and "*Everything* is just perfect" are examples of utopian self-instruction that prevent you from facing the difficult, challenging realities of daily living. Overlooking the half of the glass that is empty; exclusively concentrating on the doughnut to the neglect of the hole in it; and sweeping life's shortcomings and deficiencies under the rug are ignoring deficiencies and does not make them go away. These blemishes are best dealt with rather than denied; the phrase "out of sight, out of mind" doesn't mean "out of the way."
9. *Indiscriminate thinking* - Emotional spillover often occurs by failing to distinguish what's important from what's all-important; what is part of life from what is seen to be bigger than life. Unwanted upset is likely to

result from being unable to separate wants from needs; wishes, desires, and preferences from demands; sharing your life with someone versus sacrificing your life for someone; sadness from tragedy; involvement from entanglement; possibility from probability or inevitability; concern from consumption; wonder from worry; priority from dramatization; and disappointment from disaster. Sorting out these distinctions creates an emotional road map that more efficiently leads to a more desirable destination of clearheadedness.

10. *Other-directed views.* Consistently looking at what others are thinking and doing and then following their lead lends itself to fear, anxiety, and worry about the possibility of being out of step with one's social group. Such dependency on others is rooted in overconcern about what these others might think about you. Gullibly thinking that "If someone else said it, it must be true" does not lend itself to learning how to trust your own judgment that comes from more self-directed, independent thinking.
11. *Muddled thinking.* Overloading your thinking with too many projects at one time often will end up with you doing a little bit of a lot of things but not too much of any one thing. Biting off more than you can chew is likely to lead to a busy life but stop short of a useful life. Applying the shotgun approach to a number of simultaneous problem-solving circumstances muddies the emotional waters and prevents you from investing a fair share of creativity in any one of them. Trying to be all things to all projects discourages a solid investment in any one of these activities.
12. *Myopic perspectives.* Motivating oneself by short-range comfort and immediate convenience and advantage rather than longer range pleasure and gain is likely to lead to discovering that the pleasure of the moment more often than not leads to pain later on. Shortsightedness is perhaps the most consistent trouble-making tendency humans have. "I can't tolerate the pain that is required of me to go through to achieve a given result" is a thought that blocks a long-range view of life that asks "Do I want to feel better now or better for the rest of my life?" As

difficult as it is to face the unpleasant music of dieting, a conflict, or finishing a project, it's even more difficult in the long run not to, because the disadvantages of avoidance will pile up.

13. *Cause/effect, deterministic thinking.* Believing that events cause emotion leaves you little choice in your emotional outcomes. Presuming the inevitability of disturbance in difficult life circumstances fails to consider that if you can't change the stimulus you can still change the response. Between the stimulus (S) and the response (R) is the individual organism (O), who can mediate a more favorable emotional outcome. Such self-instructional provisions make possible the challenge often required to stubbornly resist upsetting oneself in the face of adversity. Telling yourself "I don't have to buckle under," "It's not the end of the world," and "I can see this matter through" harnesses the coping powers required to more sanely deal with a difficult situation.
14. *Defensive thoughts.* Thinking that you owe others unending explanations for your decisions and choices often results in frustration that comes from discovering that no matter what you say, it isn't what the other wants to hear. Thinking you are on trial lends itself to overexplaining which results in your putting yourself over a barrel. Consistently excusing or defensively overapologizing for yourself is not a very enjoyable way to go through life. Unashamedly saying what you mean and meaning what you say frees you up to more clearly express your messages and intentions. Directly stating "This is what I think" rather than "I'm sorry, I know it's silly, please forgive me that I think this way" is more likely to get your message heard. Too much humility will usually result in others taking you less seriously while hearing less of what you have to say more often.
15. *Personalized thinking.* Most people act on behalf of themselves rather than against others. However, when disagreement, criticism, or some other form of lack of acceptance is taken personally, one's emotional well-being is up for grabs. If other peoples' opinions or treatment of you equal you, then how others choose to relate to you determines your emotional destiny. Self-

statements such as "What's wrong with me?"; "I must have body odor or something"; and "Their bad treatment of me means I'm bad" prevent you from getting out from under giving others permission to make it convenient for you to give vent to your self-inflicted feelings of inferiority.

16. *Faulty inferences.* Arbitrarily inferring meaning behind others' negligence of you is sheer guesswork (and could make you rich in the stock market if you really possessed such a mindreading capacity!). If the boss doesn't say "Good morning" to you, it doesn't necessarily mean he or she is thinking of firing you. If someone declines your request of his or her company, it doesn't for certain represent his or her spite for you. If your associate looks at you in an out-of-the-ordinary way it doesn't absolutely indicate he or she doesn't like you. Such errors of presumption set in motion a chain of misunderstandings that, until broken, may contaminate the best intentions for future relationships.
17. *Pigeonholed, tunnel vision thinking.* Narrow-minded, rigid notions hinder brainstorming of alternatives that might better contribute to goal attainment. There are multiple ways to look at life. Dogma that pretends to have a non-negotiable monopoly on truth does not encourage the experimentation, trial-and-error learning that is frequently required to arrive at eventual helpful conclusions.
18. *Selective views.* "I'll listen to what you have to say as long as it doesn't interfere with what I've already decided to do" blocks learning from others who may think differently from you. Choosing only those ideas that are in line with your preconceived ways of thinking limits your options to those you presently hold. "Be honest - but say what I want to hear or what I already think" restricts you to the status quo, putting new, potentially helpful ideas that might go against your grain off limits.
19. *Dictatorial, demanding ideas.* "Everybody is entitled to my opinion" represents a way of thinking that attempts to establish universal laws as if there were no individuals. Words that convey the 11th commandment - "My will be done" - include "*should,*" "*must,*" "*ought to,*" "*supposed to,*" and "*got to.*" Such compelling, dichotomous, black-

or-white thinking attempts to take away free will and replace it with "my will." Insisting that circumstances and people in them "have to" be a certain way takes its emotional toll when such commands are not compatible with reality. Strive for flexible understanding by accepting that at most it may be "preferable," "better," or even "best" for matters to be a certain way. Beyond this, see that humans aren't required to do what is best, and that it is not essential that conditions be ideal. This more tolerant view will extinguish stress before it begins to simmer.

20. *Double-bind thinking.* A special form of anxiety is created when you set yourself up to be "damned if you do and damned if you don't." Exhorting yourself to do what you believe yourself to be duty bound to do tends to leave you on the emotional hot seat regardless of the choice you make. Obligating yourself to go to church or visit grandmother because you believe it to be mandatory leaves you (a) feeling angry if you go in that some arbitrary authority is suggesting you "have to" go, and (b) feeling guilty if you don't go for violating this all-inclusive code of conduct. Being more permissive with yourself by asking "What do I really want to do?" and then freely making that choice will loosen up the self-imposed tie that you bind yourself with.
21. *Namby-pamby expressions.* Causing yourself to feel undisciplined and lethargic by convincing yourself that the world is indeed too tough discourages constructive effort before you get started. Declarations such as "I just can't stand it," "It's wretched," "It's unwieldy," "It's out of this world," "It's mortifying," and "It's much too much to take" result in emotional pampering that runs counter to productive action.
22. *Oppositional thoughts.* Looking at what others, especially those in authority, are doing or telling you to do (and then doing the opposite) often results in "cutting off your nose to spite your face." Such self-defeating reactions to others' lead, often with the mentality of "I'll show them," are likely to return and haunt your best interests. Different versions of nagging dissenting behavior are likely to produce similar regret after consequences that stem from "throwing the baby out with the bath water."

23. *Bigoted thoughts.* Bigotry means evaluating someone or someone else's behavior as different and then concluding that (a) "It's different so therefore it must be bad," and (b) "If the situation is bad then the people in it must be too." Believing that people with certain characteristics, traits, or features (especially those that are unusual) are of lesser value than those who do not possess these same aspects shows narrow-minded bias. Rating people as good or bad because of something about them is the essence of prejudice. Rating yourself by one or more of your flaws will get you down on self; judging others by this itemizing procedure gets you down on them.
24. *Superstitious notions.* Running your emotional life by superstitious whims rather than facts leaves emotional wellness to fate and chance. Believing that certain things are "meant to be" or "bound to happen" fails to distinguish what *could* happen from what is *bound* to happen. Inventing dramatic moments - such as in beliefs that "The first time I see my former mate after our divorce I'll be devastated," "When my youngest leaves home I'll be lost," or "My first day of retirement will be a shock" puts response possibilities beyond your control. Other examples of predetermined, emotionally shattering ways of thinking are: "Mondays are bad" and "Winters, Christmases, and anniversaries are hard on me." Believing "Good always wins out over evil so if I do something good, noble, or angelic I'm bound to get good in return" encourages anxiety and self-pity if you don't. Expecting that certain rituals will ward off calamity (such as getting out of bed on one side only, not stepping on cracks, wearing certain clothes on certain days) and believing that forgetting these repetitive tasks will cause dastardly things to occur promotes worry about the assumed negative happening. Another self-inflicted scare tactic that there is no evidence for is "Just when it seems that things are going okay - watch out." Assuming that when you err some sort of atonement or penance is required to perfume your mistake will likely result in you being your own whipping person following inevitable blunders.
25. *Magical thinking.* Most people assume that people and circumstances magically get inside them and cause their

feelings. Such automatic ways of thinking create the illusion that feelings magically evolve beyond an individual's control. Examples of phrases that attribute feelings to mystical forces are: "*It* scared me." "*It* seems to work out that way; isn't that the way *it* always goes?" (rather than "I make it go"). "I *get* overwhelmed by *it*." "*It*'s been that kind of day." "I *got* or *was given* those beliefs" (rather than invented my own). "*Things* build up." "I *become* upset" (rather than "I encourage myself to feel upset"). "He *makes me* angry." "*That* was the last straw." "*It* all depends on how *it* goes." "Where does *that* leave me?" "That *gets* to me." These terms leave you searching for magical forces such as "it" in an unclear attempt to better understand yourself and your emotions. Assuming that you have little say-so in determining your feelings leaves you a helpless hostage to forces beyond your control.

26. *Mandatory thinking.* Trapping yourself by assigning arbitrary definitions for happiness and survival puts all your emotional eggs in one basket. This hazardous manner of thinking results in bottomless emotional pits, whether what you've defined as a "need" is delivered or not. Identifying wants and wishes for love, achievement, acceptance, and approval as needs and requirements encourages a sense of desperation whether the well is full or not. How much is full enough when one puts this infinite way of thinking into gear? For example, thinking that you "need" love is likely to create a feeling of starvation and exasperation, making you as lovable as a wet mop and driving others away. After all, who needs a needy person?
27. *Condemning, judgmental thinking.* Getting after people's behavior, acknowledging their shortcomings, and holding them accountable for faults and errors is one thing; condemning and judging them for and by those same flaws is another. Seeing that people have a right to be wrong, that they are wrong in being wrong (don't get me wrong), counters the tendency to think that you are anointed to damn self and others for mutual imperfections. Unfortunately, to err is human, and to blame is even more human.

The chart on pages 174 to 179 reviews and structures the varying types of thinking and categorizes specific self-sentences that cause unwanted disturbed emotions. Then contrasting ideas are presented to assist you in feeling more the way you want to feel and less the way you don't want to feel.

Alternative ways of helping yourself to feel more the way you want to feel and less the way you don't want to feel might include the following:

1. *Scientific thinking.* Ask yourself "Where's the evidence?" or "Where is the proof?" regarding your hypothesis; this is perhaps the surest way to keep your thinking aligned with reality. If there are no factual data to support your premise, it's best for you to get rid of it lest you lead your life by falsehoods that are likely to cause you more harm than good.

   In rational-emotive theory there are three basic ideas that lay the groundwork for emotional disturbance. None of these three irrational beliefs has supportive, provable documentation. Because these ideas do not stand the test of scientific inquiry, a rational-emotive therapist goes about the business of encouraging his or her clients to give them up. The three unscientific, unverifiable ideas believed to be fundamental to emotional upsettedness are (a) I *have to* do perfectly well, (b) others *have to* treat me perfectly kindly and gently, and (c) life *has to* be perfectly fair and partial to me. Although it would be nice, preferable, and desirable if things and people were a certain way, there is no evidence that anything or anyone in life has to be as such.
2. *Consequential thinking.* Looking at the results of your actions and deciding if you wish to continue along the same outcome lines permits you to be more your own traffic director of future experiences. This technique of evaluating your own behavior can be done by saying to yourself, "This is the result of my conducting myself in such a manner; do I want to continue to conduct myself in this way and experience similar outcomes, or do I want to change my actions and perhaps obtain better results?"

3. *Long-range thinking.* Ask yourself "Do I want to feel better now or do I want to feel better for the rest of my life?" This will allow you to consider not only immediate gains but also a more expanded calculation of your profits and losses. Opting for choices that in the long run are likely to provide you with more pleasure and less pain require you to look at matters in a way that goes beyond decision making that is merely immediately convenient.
4. *Panoramic, lateral thinking.* For a broader view, permit yourself to see the forest rather than just a few trees. Looking to all sides rather than just straight ahead poses fuller consideration of all the pieces in the problem-solving puzzle.
5. *Situational-specific thinking.* Confront yourself with the question "How is this situation different from any other I've encountered?" This makes it convenient for you to bring a unique perspective to each situation you deal with. Rather than force your foot to fit the shoe, it would be better to make the shoe fit the foot. That way, creative, well-thought-out solutions are likely to be the rule rather than the exception.
6. *Flexible thinking.* Leaving the door open for the possibility of change fits into the spirit of scientific documentation. Science is tentative, flexible, and ever-changing. Seeing that the world is ever-changing, and that very few people in it stay the same, flexibly accommodates these realities. Statements such as "so far," "up until now," and "up to this point" introduce the possibility that as new evidence presents itself tomorrow can be different from today.
7. *Optional thinking.* Allowing your mind to play by brainstorming alternative ways of looking at old problems increases opportunities for constructive action. Piggybacking one idea on another can help even further to produce potential solutions. Seeing that there are many methods for solving problems builds hope and self-encouragement en route to sampling your smorgasbord of choices.
8. *Tolerant thinking.* Accepting people and things as they are has its advantages. Learning how to live with the reality of not getting what you want or getting what you

don't want readies you for the curve balls that life will not infrequently throw at you. Acceptance of disappointments in self, others, and life conditions is a major change in the direction of lightening up on yourself about matters that, for the present, can't be changed.

9. *Self-inspired, self-directed, individualistic thinking.* Taking your cue from yourself rather than from others reflects the belief that no other person or group of other people knows more about what's best for you than you. Making your own independent choices allows you to be your own best teacher in living with, and learning from, the outcomes of your choices. Depending less on others to find answers to your life's questions frees you up to do more research on the questions themselves.

What's in a word? Plenty! Words are the substance out of which emotions are made. Humans tend to feel the way they think and then act the way they feel. They bring themselves to their behavior or block themselves from their behavior by how they think. Feelings do not spontaneously erupt. People create, maintain, and eliminate their feeling states largely by how and what they think. Learning a method of thinking that helps you to feel more the way you want to feel and less the way you don't want to feel is a comprehensive investment. Educator John Holt said that we are not very good at figuring out what it is important for us to learn. Because humans have feelings about practically everything they do, what could be better than to learn precise, accurate means of interpreting happenings in a way that assists in experiencing life more fully and favorably?

Precision in saying what you mean and meaning what you say is a significant tool in exercising responsibility for your own mental health. You have the capacity to tune up or tune down what is uniquely human - feelings. Guiding yourself by your self-instructional ideas under an umbrella of realism and temperedness rather than beyond reality and extremism makes for a fuller, more energizing existence.

A male kindergarten student said to his female teacher: "Me slept with Daddy last night." The teacher corrected back: "No, I slept with Daddy last night." The youngster then countered with: "Then it must have been after me fell asleep." The moral of that story and this guide: Be careful of the words that you use. Not fanning the flames of emotional disturbance by feeding it bonfire words will not make for a heavenly, happy life in itself, but it is unlikely that you will have a consistently satisfying one without such deliberating language.

TYPES OF THINKING	EXAMPLES OF THOUGHTS THAT CAUSE DISTURBANCE		EXAMPLES OF CONTRASTING THOUGHTS THAT HELP WITH EMOTIONAL SELF-CONTROL
1. Finalistic	"Things *always* go wrong."	→	"*Sometimes* things go wrong."
	"*Every time* I try I fail."	→	"*Frequently* I have been failing."
	"Things *never* work out."	→	"*Often* things haven't been working out."
2. Overgeneralizing	"*All* men (women) are untrustworthy."	→	"*Some* people, *sometimes* are best not trusted."
	"I *am* a failure/stupid."	→	"I'm a person who *sometimes* fails/acts stupidly."
	"This is *bigger* than life."	→	"This is an *important* part of my life, at most."
3. Catastrophic, Overreactive	"*How awful*."	→	"This is *disappointing*."
	"This is *overwhelming*."	→	"This is *difficult*."
4. Fictional	"Life *has to be* fair; this *shouldn't* have happened."	→	"I *wish* life were fairer than it actually is, though sometimes I'm glad it isn't."
			"This *should have* happened because it did."
5. Qualifying	"*Maybe* I will."	→	"I've *decided* to do it."
	"I *might*."	→	"I *will* do it."

6. Hedging	"I *guess* I'll finish."	→	"I'm *going to* finish what I started."
	"I'm *pretty sure* I will."		
7. Underreactive	"Who cares."	→	"It'd be best if I cared less without becoming uncaring."
	"It makes *no* difference."	→	"It does make a difference, just not an all-or-nothing cne."
8. Wonderfulizing	"Life is perfect." "*Everything* is super."	→	"*Many things* are presently working out for me."
	"Thinking positively is *the* answer to making it so."	→	"Thinking *doesn't* make it so, but my working hard might."
9. Indiscriminate	"This matter is *all important*."	→	"This matter is important but *not* sacred."
	"This is something to be *consumed* about."	→	"It would be important to be *concerned* and *involved* but *nct* consumed and entangled."
10. Other-Directed	"*Others* know more about what is best for me than me."	→	"I know what's best for me."
	"What *other* people think is more important than what I think."	→	What *I think* is more important to me than what others think."

TYPES OF THINKING	EXAMPLES OF THOUGHTS THAT CAUSE DISTURBANCE	EXAMPLES OF CONTRASTING THOUGHTS THAT HELP WITH EMOTIONAL SELF-CONTROL
11. Muddled	"I have to do and understand *everything at once*." →	"One step at a time."
		"Don't get ahead of yourself."
		"Busy is *not* a substitute for being useful."
12. Myopic	"If it feels good *now* do it." →	"It's best that I do what is going to bring me more pleasure in the *long run*."
		"Short-range pain for long-range gain."
		"Do I want to feel better now or better for the rest of my life?"
13. Cause/Effect, Deterministic	"What happened earlier *caused* what I feel now." →	"I *affect myself* more than I'm affected."
		"I *script myself* more than I'm scripted."
		"I *condition myself* more than I'm conditioned."
14. Defensive, On Guard	"I *have to get* others to understand me." →	"Others' understanding or acceptance is *not* essential."
	"PRETTY PLEASE, forgive me." →	"I apologize."

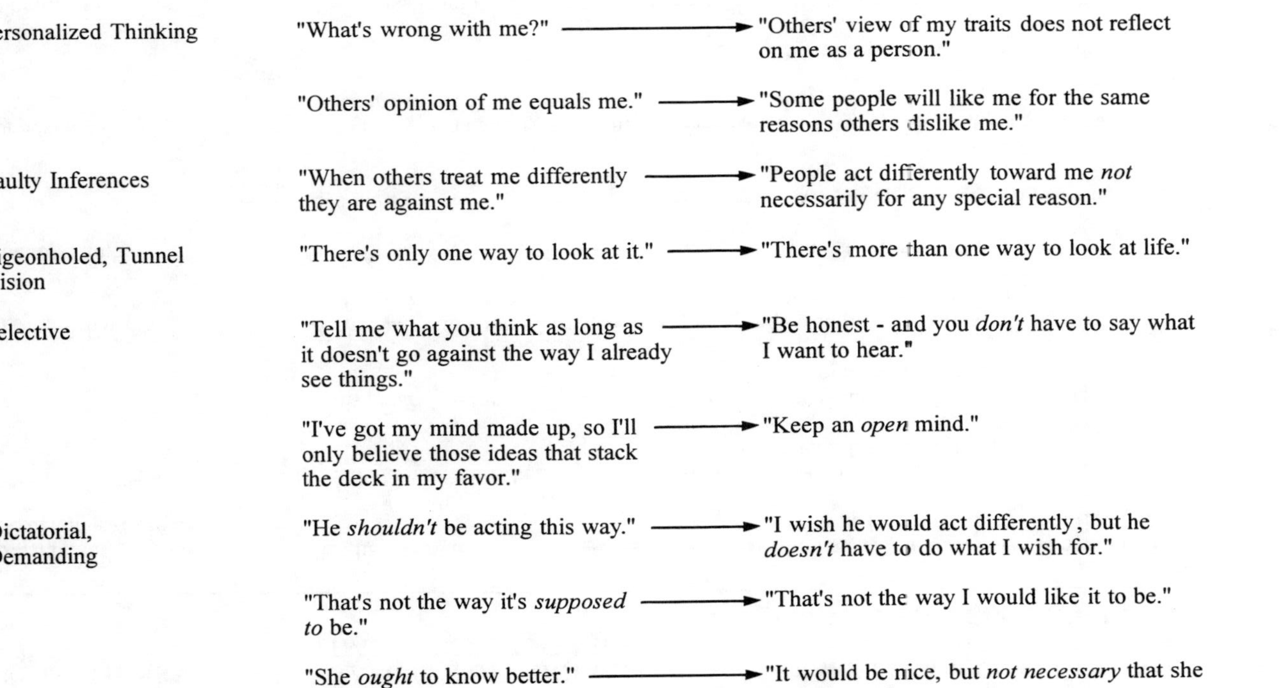

15. Personalized Thinking	"What's wrong with me?" →	"Others' view of my traits does not reflect on me as a person."
	"Others' opinion of me equals me." →	"Some people will like me for the same reasons others dislike me."
16. Faulty Inferences	"When others treat me differently they are against me." →	"People act differently toward me *not* necessarily for any special reason."
17. Pigeonholed, Tunnel Vision	"There's only one way to look at it." →	"There's more than one way to look at life."
18. Selective	"Tell me what you think as long as it doesn't go against the way I already see things." →	"Be honest - and you *don't* have to say what I want to hear."
	"I've got my mind made up, so I'll only believe those ideas that stack the deck in my favor." →	"Keep an *open* mind."
19. Dictatorial, Demanding	"He *shouldn't* be acting this way." →	"I wish he would act differently, but he *doesn't* have to do what I wish for."
	"That's not the way it's *supposed to* be." →	"That's not the way I would like it to be."
	"She *ought* to know better." →	"It would be nice, but *not necessary* that she know better."

TYPES OF THINKING	EXAMPLES OF THOUGHTS THAT CAUSE DISTURBANCE	EXAMPLES OF CONTRASTING THOUGHTS THAT HELP WITH EMOTIONAL SELF-CONTROL
19. Dictatorial, Demanding *(Cont'd)*	"He has no right." →	"*He has a right* to follow his own mind, though I wish he hadn't exercised that right!"
	"I *should* have done better." →	"I would have preferred to do better but instead I did what I could."
	"This *should* be easier." →	"I wish this were easier, but often things that are good for me aren't - tough, too bad!"
20. Double-Bind	"I *have to* go to church" or "I *should* visit grandma's." →	"I would like to (or would like not to) go to church (or visit grandma's)."
21. Namby-Pamby	"I *can't* stand it." →	"I *can* stand what I don't like."
	"It's *unbearable*." →	"I *can* put up with anything as long as I'm alive."
22. Oppositional	"I'll get my revenge; whatever he wants me to do, I'll do just the opposite." →	"Do I want to spite the other person or do what is better for myself?"
		"Bittersweet revenge - who needs it."
23. Bigoted	"Because she thinks and acts differently than me, she's no good." →	"Different means different, *not* bad."

24.	Superstitious	"It was *meant* to be." →	"Things sometimes happen for *no* special reason."
		"It's *bound to* happen."	
		"The universe runs in orderly cycles."	
25.	Magical	"*It* upset me." →	"I upset myself about it."
		"That's the way *it* goes." →	"That's the way I *make it* go."
		"*I got upset!*" →	"I encouraged myself to feel upset."
		"*Things* build up." →	"I build things up."
26.	Mandatory	"I *need* him." →	"I *want*/desire/prefer him but don't need what I want."
		"I *require* certain things to go my way before I can feel happy." →	"It would be nice to do well, but nice *doesn't* mean necessary."
		"I need to succeed."	
27.	Condemning, Judgmental	"I am to be blamed." →	"I am at fault but am *not* to be blamed."
		"She stinks!" →	"She's not perfect either."
		"The world stinks!" →	"I better do myself a favor and get used to the smell."

The Operation Wasn't a Success and the Patient Lived: Feeling Transplants as Futility

"The road to Hell is paved with good intentions," goes the saying. Likewise, good intentions not backed by the right methods spell frustration if one's goal is to take on another's emotional hurt. Such efforts are futile because no one has invented a way to transfer feelings. Magical thinking presumes such transplants are not only possible but required as representative of one's caring nature. This narrow definition of caring often accompanies such presumed obligation: "If you love someone you are duty bound to take on his upset, and if you fail to do so this means you love him less." Such rigid other-saving ideas actually (a) are not so much acts of love, because one of the most loving things you can do for people is not take them as seriously as they take themselves, and (b) further contribute to an already heightened emotional climate; unwanted emotions multiply because now there are two people who are emotionally overcharged.

Examples of loved ones' hurt that can't be taken on include:

- A child who didn't survive the last cut of the school's basketball team.
- A colleague who got passed over for promotion.
- A friend whose partner broke off their engagement.

- Parents who were informed that their child was picked up for shoplifting.
- A family member who is mourning the loss of a person, project, or ambition.
- A relative who just lost a child at birth.
- Neighbors who lost their home because they couldn't keep up the mortgage payments.
- A waiter who is being publicly criticized by his boss.
- A client who lapsed into a deep depression.
- An instructor who was recently told her contract wouldn't be renewed.
- A favorite performer who, because of factors beyond his control, cannot continue to stay with his profession.

If these individuals were hurt in a car accident or were having a tooth pulled, you could not shield them from their own feeling experiences. Acknowledging this reality is not a breach of loyalty but a reach toward acceptance. Cultivating a sense of humility for what you can and cannot do for significant others allows you to not make a bad situation worse. Attempts to take on or talk others out of their feelings are a lost cause and promote your feeling sorry for them. Such pity is not beneficial and encourages a one-down attitude on the one who has the disadvantage.

Adversity can stimulate advantages if you play your cards right. Good intentions backed up by the following right ideas and methods in responding to important others' unpleasant plights can permit you to set boundaries on emotional empathy. Also, the circumstances can be bent so as to work to the advantage of the "me, you, and us" components of your relationship.

Try out the following suggestions and see if you can make them work for you in better assuring a successful problem-solving operation - where "the patient lives" to experience the satisfaction of taking more responsibility for his or her own emotional life.

1. *Avoid unsolicited advice.* Like lead balloons, suggestions provided in the absence of requests don't go very far. Until someone gives you a definite go-ahead, well-intended suggestions are likely to fall on deaf ears.

2. *Avoid pitying others.* Feeling sorry for another will give you a depression similar to the one you are concerned about in the other. Such mutual distress is best avoided in the service of clearheaded problem solving.
3. *Understand others' active participation in their own upset.* People are not the passive victims of their feelings; so too they had best be the active participants of their emotional self-control. Magical thinking says that people are given emotions. Scientific views hold that people create, maintain, and minimize unwanted feelings.
4. *Emotional free will versus manifest destiny.* Take on a view that recognizes free will rather than determinism. See that the more permissive and less hovering you make yourself in not attempting to save other people from themselves the more encouraging you will be to them in gaining a better grip on exercising their emotional recharging.
5. *Exercise humility.* Take on a nonordained perspective. Accept that you have not been assigned the position of general manager of the universe and thus are not charged with finding solutions to others' problems. Graciously see what you can and cannot do for a fellow human. Accept that such acknowledgement is a humane thing to do and that it would be inhumane to undermine other's problem-solving potential by trying to do their work for them.
6. *Develop a democratic view of suffering.* People have a right to and can find advantage to their suffering. To insist otherwise (e.g., "He shouldn't feel that way," "I have to find a way to make her happy") is undemocratic. The philosopher Nietzsche saw being worthy of his suffering to be an asset. Given the opportunity to not be emotionally smothered in the midst of bleak circumstances, people can often learn from and independently rise above such adversity.
7. *Extend the benefits.* Out of restraint in the face of another's distress can rise benefits of increased tolerance levels for yourself and votes of confidence for the other.
8. *Focus on the advantages.* What you learn from the school of hard knocks is likely to be remembered longer. What you learn from what feels bad now can be put to

use in future similar circumstances. Call to mind the often-required "present pain for future gain" to provide a longer range, more well-rounded view of present disappointments.

9. *See that emotions are often time limited.* With the exception of worry, which sticks like a stamp, most emotions will naturally run their course. True, they are likely to move along more quickly if you get after the notions that set them off. However, merely letting time pass without the interference that comes from getting yourself emotionally entangled in the web of others' disturbances may likely be enough medicine to let the wound heal.
10. *Redefine caring.* Understand a healthy concern to be not smothering entanglement but rather expecting more of people than they expect of themselves. Not treating someone like an emotional cripple will likely activate the other's problem-solving resources.
11. *See sadness as healthy and beneficial.* To feel sad means you're alive and willfully and wellfully absorbed in life. Sadness had best not be discouraged as it allows one to more finely appreciate one's values. Before considering being of assistance be clear on what the other is up against emotionally. Sadness or regret is not depression. In some ways, if people weren't feeling sad in the throes of adversity, they might be having even bigger problems!
12. *Ask, don't tell.* Before you try to save the other's day by sharing with him or her your bottomless reservoir of noble advice, ask him or her what sort of a problem-solving plan he or she is considering. After asking "What's your plan?" (rather than telling "Here's my plan") you may find the other doesn't have one. This being so, suggest: "Think further about this matter and when you come up with some ideas let me know, because I'm interested." Expecting the other to think through his or her options, while explaining that your spoon-feeding solutions to the problems isn't going to make him or her a better problem solver, may go a long way toward demonstrating a caring option. It invites and encourages another's self-sufficiency.
13. *Remember three little words.* Actively understanding another's emotions without trying to transplant them is a

very practical way to make it convenient for the other to come to terms with his or her problems. Demonstrating your awareness of what it feels like to walk a mile in another's moccasins is likely to work to mutual advantage both in the relationship between the helper and helpee and in the latter's ability to handle his or her problems. "I understand you" messages can be conveyed through the following empathic response leads:

- "It sounds like you feel. . . ."
- "It seems that this is a difficult time for you."
- "My guess is that was disappointing for you."
- "I sense that you're feeling. . . ."
- "It sounds as if you're indicating feelings of. . . ."
- "In listening to you it seems as if you're feeling. . . ."
- "Is it true that you're conveying a sense of. . . ."
- "If I'm hearing you correctly, you feel. . . ."
- "To me it's almost as if you're saying, 'I feel. . . .' "
- "The message that I get from you is that you're feeling. . . ."

14. *Develop powerful countering coping ideas.* List strong coping statements that reflect tolerance, reality, and acceptance of that reality in relation to another's problems and disturbance. Then, state these ideas to yourself daily, preferably out loud, to get the rational message across in your and the other's best interests. Examples are:

    - "I'm *not* responsible for others' problems; this proven fact does *not* mean I love them less."
    - "Care less without becoming uncaring."
    - "Witnessing another's problems is sad but not unbearable."
    - "Every problem doesn't have to have a solution, and I don't have to look for something that may be nowhere to be found."
    - "Take a step back rather than two steps forward."
    - "I can't save people from themselves."
    - "I'll try to understand, but I don't have to do the best in taking care of a matter that only she can."

- "Sometimes the solution to a problem is to accept that there is no solution."
- "I can't reason someone out of a problem that he probably hasn't reasoned himself into."
- "Stay concerned but don't make yourself consumed."
- "Remain deliberately involved but don't cause yourself to be desperately entangled."

What constitutes a good emotional Samaritan? The implication of this guide is that it is someone who knows when *not* to operate; someone who knows more about what *not* to do rather than somebody who thinks he or she knows what is best for the other more than the other knows what's best for himself or herself. Feelings can't be given to or taken away from someone else. If this were possible we could provide each other happy feelings forever. This realization of transplant limitations avoids trying to accomplish the impossible mission of saving people from themselves; allowing the "patients" to live on under the advantages of their own resources.

How to Avoid Letting Others' Opinions Get Under Your Skin

"Sticks and stones will break your bones but words will never harm you" - (unless you sharpen them up and stick them in yourself). Unfortunately, the human thing to do is to take others' opinions personally by sharpening them up and then using them against your emotional well-being. By the same token, such thin-skinned responses are inhumane in that you commit an act of hurt against a human being - yourself. Such instances of immoral conduct can be avoided by giving yourself more clearheaded understanding of what others' negative reviews of you really demonstrate. The topic of this guide is how to not treat others' words as magic; how to not let them get under your skin.

Typically, when criticized, humans respond in two ways: (a) "What's wrong with me that I can't gain another's liking and get the other to treat me better? What a bad person I must be for being treated so badly." This is a normal but unhealthy response to another's bias. It would be best for you to review the variety of other possibilities as to why you may be targeted for negative comments. (b) "What's wrong with me? What a louse I must be for not coping more favorably with another's disfavor." Insisting that you be the rock of Gibraltar, unaffected by another's views of you, makes it convenient for you to put yourself down when not being able to do so perfectly. Ideas such as "I have to be able to cope perfectly well - or else I'm perfectly worthless" will help you create problems about the original problem. These self-put-downs on two fronts create the hurt that comes from taking another's words - and your own inability to cope with them more effectively - too seriously.

A better question to ask yourself might be: "What does it really mean that my associate is taking the time to strongly draw attention to what he views as my deficiencies?" There are many beliefs that aim at distinguishing another's opinion as being apart from you. All have in common the idea that nobody can demean you but you. Only you can discredit yourself by taking another's disfavor and trampling yourself by using it to devalue yourself. An answer to the previous question might be "Unfortunately, my contrary-acting associate apparently has got nothing better to do than to try to hassle me. What a miserable existence he must lead. Let me see if I can figure out a way to protect myself from his deplorable actions without judging myself by them."

The suggestions that follow reflect the notion that others' estimates of you are just that - skin-deep appraisals that are best not seen as being indicators of your value to yourself. Rather, others' overdone reviews could expose any of the following:

1. *Their values (what is important to them).* Criticizing something about you may be your adversaries' way of affirming their values. However aggressively firm their views might be, understand that their ideas and emotions reflect what they prize in life; they do not stigmatize you.
2. *Their disturbance.* The higher the intensity of others' negative comments, the more godlike they are likely to see them, and the more disturbed these commanding-acting people are likely to be. Their warlike approach to their dislike mirrors their inability to take the sacredness out of their values.
3. *Their limitations.* People who act critically in a nonconstructive way are short-sighted because of their bias. Taking on a broader world view, which would enable them to act more tolerantly, seems to be beyond their reach.

4. *Their tastes and preferences.* Beauty is often in the eyes of the beholder. Selecting against you for reasons of fashion need not be viewed as even a close call in reflecting you.
5. *Their ignorance.* Having never been taught principles of individual differences, appreciation of human variability may be a concept foreign to them.
6. *Their stupidity.* Although exposed to the idea that each human being is an experiment of one, they may not have allowed such a broad-minded notion to take hold. Innate learning deficiencies may prevent such a permissive view to penetrate.

Use the preceding attribution self-help concepts to learn to realize what others' conduct toward you tells you about them rather than assuming their actions tell you much about you. In addition, use the following suggestions to close the seemingly automatic floodgates of self-depreciation, hurt, and anger that often are made to follow another's negative appraisal.

1. *Distinguish practical dependency from emotional dependency.* You depend on others for certain practical advantages (e.g., your employer to write your checks, your friends to socialize, your teacher for a passing grade, your mate to reliably fulfill his or her domestic roles). However, emotional dependency is excess baggage. Convince yourself that others' decisions about you may adversely affect you in practical ways, but they aren't the least bit related to your potential to accept yourself. With this belief you will likely loosen up rather than think you will lose yourself in matters of others' nonacceptance of you.
2. *Avoid the following misery equations.* (a) "Others' opinions equal me." This puts your emotional comfort up for grabs in that you let others' thinking about you determine how you feel. (b) "My deficiencies equal me." Here again, external props are defined as a requirement for emotional self-fulfillment. If I falter in gaining liking in the first place, and then experience myself to be deficient at coping with disapproval in the second place, by this

brand of report-card logic I have a double-barreled reason to get down on myself.

3. *No magic.* Understand that no matter how much you upset yourself over others' bigotry your emotions are unlikely to magically change their discriminatory views. What is more likely to happen is that your own brand of overreaction will recertify their negative opinion. Your dramatics will likely, in their own mind, prove their point (e.g., "The bad way she responded to me demonstrated what I already knew").
4. *Avoid "I-can't-stand-it-itis."* Up your tolerance level for harsh comments and your sometimes regretful twice-baked response to them. As you convince yourself that you can stand what you don't like, you will take pressure off yourself and in doing so demonstrate to others that you are not going to do yourself in emotionally by overreacting to their comments. This will discourage them from such future criticisms.
5. *Put in a different context.* Welcome others' criticism in the sense that it provides you with an opportunity to work on building a case for emotional self-control and self-acceptance in the face of adversity. Seize this option for the good of increasing your tolerance and self-acceptance.
6. *See that others are for themselves and not against you.* When others thwart you they ordinarily have their best interest at heart. People are mainly *for their* advantages rather than *against you.* Understanding this will assist you in lightening the load of taking it personally.
7. *Emphasize individual tastes.* Some people will like you for the same reasons that others don't. Most of what is taken personally reflects one person's poison - which may be another person's cup of tea. The poison does not degrade you nor does the tea exalt you.
8. *Cushion your surprise.* Question: "How can he think that way about me?" Answer: "Easily!" Humans at times very naturally vent their frustrations on even those they love the most. Expecting and accepting this more than occasional grim reality makes it less tempting to sharpen up those words that only you can harm yourself with.

9. *Uninvent the reverse golden rule.* The faulty notion that others should do unto you as you do unto them had best go by the boards. Such score keeping implies that the world of relationships runs in orderly cycles. Regardless of how much you welcome your associates, they will not necessarily refrain from exercising their choice to treat you with gaps in kindness and consideration. Childish demands for a return on your investment of gratitude will make you even less fun to be around for an associate who already views his or her relationship with you in a dim light.
10. *View rejection and put-downs as self-inflicted.* What you can inflict you can uninflict. When people don't like something about you they are really selecting against you. When you observe their bias and conclude "Because my acquaintance voices bad reviews of me, I'm bad," rejection occurs. No one but you can put you down - and you can decide that you have better things to do.
11. *If not with you, then with someone else.* Others' unflattering comments are often interchangeable. In a similar situation, your nemesis is likely to treat anyone else the same. This vision provides added logic against the advisability of taking the other too seriously. Is the next person your foe treats badly to be rated a sinister individual because he or she has sinned against your adversary's values?
12. *Traits, characteristics, and features as dimensions, not entities.* Distinguishing the things that one has or does from oneself shields much emotional disturbance. This dividing line often constitutes the boundary between sanity and disturbance. Even strong criticism can only give negative review to aspects of your manner and personality. Those skin-deep portions do not make up your essence, which is too complex to judge. It is not possible to legitimately rate a person in total as "good" or "bad" because of people's multidimensional natures. What can be judged are only those parts that stand out in an attractive or unattractive way (in the eyes of the beholder).
13. *Ask yourself: "What do others really owe me?"* Self-pity in the face of discrimination can be warded off by realiz-

ing others aren't required to accept your nature as it fails to accommodate their values. Others are not duty bound to make the adjustments that would be required to fit their likes with what they dislike about you.

14. *Others' intensity as it best encourages your acceptance.* The stronger the other thinks in contrary ways about you, the more justification you have for accepting what can't be changed. Another's hard and fast rules that portray his or her dislike toward you are best seen as a tip-off toward a determined acceptance of what exists and what, in good probability, will continue to exist.
15. *Energizing, persistent coping statements.* Strongly and repeatedly telling yourself coping ideas that reflect self-acceptance and acceptance of reality can be quite helpful in keeping other's opinions about you from getting under your skin. These include:

- "Others' opinions reflect their views, they don't reflect on me."
- "I may desire another's approval, but I certainly don't require such liking."
- "I can live, survive, and be happy preferably with, but also regretfully without, another's acclaim."
- "I can look to myself for emotional strength and direction - I don't need a weather forecaster to know which way the wind is blowing."
- "Others can dissatisfy and inconvenience me - but they can't diminish me."
- "Because another's acceptance is not a life-or-death matter I can afford to be myself without thinking that I am required to prove myself."
- "Virtually nothing in life has to be - including others' shining up to me."
- "Another's favorable review is nice, but hardly necessary, and certainly not sacred."
- "When I associate with others it often may be important that they review me favorably, but such positive appraisal is definitely not all-important."
- "Because others pass judgment on me does not mean that I have to do a number on myself. In fact, when

others send my way unfavorable, unfair estimates of me, this is all the more reason for me to build a case for being more fair to myself."

When others discover what they believe to be a flaw in your character or performance, examine their inference closely. If their negative critique hits the nail of your fallible nature on the head, work hard to correct your fault. If you don't take accurate constructive criticism seriously you are likely to disadvantage yourself by this oversight. However, don't assume their criticism to be sacred or even gospel; understand that opinions are often a matter of preference. In either case, whether you view their judgment as correct or incorrect, make strenuous efforts to convince yourself that their views don't represent you. See that what you think of yourself is more important than what others think of you.

The poet Emily Dickinson said "The tie between us is very small, but a hair never dissolves." Choose not to live your life on a shoestring by making your acceptance of yourself dependent upon others' acceptance of you. Instead, realize the tie between your self-acceptance and your emotional well-being may be very small, but your self-accepting beliefs never have to be dissolved.

I've Got the Fever, But Do You Really Have the Cure? Love Dependency: Complexities, Complications, And Corrections

People have some funny ideas about love that are quite sad. Many of these faulty notions are based on:

1. *The short-range convenience of staying in a love relationship even when it is more harmful than not.* Much of what is called "love addiction" is really a self-created dependency on immediate comfort. When the adjustment process of leaving an unsatisfying relationship is viewed as being more difficult than staying in it, the status quo becomes the pathway of choice. Those who opt for this line of least resistance will do so until the immediate pain of everyday incompatibility outweighs the fear of the long-range unknown. Matters are allowed to get worse before they get better before realizing that frustration doesn't have to mount before taking forward-looking action. Fear of immediate discomfort and shortsightedness result in attachment to the rush of instant relief that is experienced from putting off until tomorrow what has already been put off until today. Love junkies are really comfort junkies in disguise. Exaggerating the pain that is required to leave a dead-end relationship while basking in the short-run security of maintaining the familiar does not allow a dead relationship to get a decent burial.

2. *Self-judgments in proportion to the quality of one's love life.* Measuring oneself as favorable when among the very loving and as unfavorable when on the outside looking in to love possibilities leads to emotional entrapment. Without a love baseline you are likely to depress yourself about lacking the necessary prop to increase your self-estimation. With love in hand, anxiety about being without your sacred measure that would lead to self-diminishment is likely to dominate.
3. *Unquestioning reliance on commercialized platitudes.* These sound comforting but come up short in the midst of everyday elbow-rubbing realities. It is as if believers of the Hollywood drama don't want to be told the truth about love, even though the truth would mean the freedom to think and to choose in a more flexible, well-thought-out manner what foundation they would like to lay for intimate relationships.
4. *Mistaken ideas about what love or lack of it can or cannot do to and for a person.* All-or-nothing beliefs that love can either build you up or tear you down put you at the mercy of one dimension of your life and block a more well-rounded view of self.

People raise their emotional temperatures for these described reasons: temporary convenience, self-evaluation, gullibility to media's unrealistic portrayals, and absolute expectations regarding love's advantages. Consequently they expose themselves to such emotional hazards as fear, anger, guilt, and depression. Matters are then made more complicated by the practical disadvantages of driving others away. Desperate, upset people are not much fun to be around, and often they find that they do not blend well with those whom they wish to become closer to. Although they longingly look to others to supply the cure for the dependency that ails them, their other-directed methods defeat the purpose of their good intentions. They rightly form attachments and then wrongly rely on exclusive return attachments to support their original investment. Finding little value in themselves, they look to others to supply their emotional fix.

To moderate love's passion made dependent, let's examine the ways of thinking that trigger such rising heartfelt temperatures. Such an overview has the advantage of building one's love relationships on the rock of self-sufficiency rather than on the sand of dependence on others. Following is a list of 26 irrational ideas about love. "Irrational" is defined as notions that cannot be verified with evidence. Each irrational belief (IB) is followed by (a) a faulty self-statement (FSS) that tries to document the thought but leads to interfering emotions (IE); (b) countering self-statements (CSS) that argue against the original unprovable idea so as to lead to more favorable feelings (FF); and (c) general comment (GC) about the rational background philosophy of each manner of thinking, feeling, and acting.

1. IB: *Love is a dire need that unless met will create utter and profound misery.*
   FSS: "I need love and therefore would be devastated without it."
   IE: Fear, anxiety.
   CSS: (a) "Love may be one of the nicest things that I could experience, but nice doesn't mean necessary"; (b) "True, I would feel sad without love in my life but I wouldn't have to turn that disappointment into a disaster"; (c) "There is evidence that I very much want love but there is no universal truth that says it is a requirement for my life."
   FF: Healthy concern and anticipation.
   GC: Striving for what you value in life is the substance out of which much meaning is created. Thinking that you have to have (need) what you find highly desirable takes you from being vitally involved in pursuing love's advantages to becoming emotionally entangled in gaining what you prize. Consequently, you will likely clumsily defeat your own purposes while driving others away with your desperation.

2. IB: *Love is a valid indicator of personal worth.*
   FSS: "Love increases my self-worth and makes me a better and good person (while being without it decreases my self-worth and makes me a worse and a bad person)."
   IE: Depression, guilt.

CSS: (a) "In some ways love results in my being better off, but having love's advantages does not turn me into a better person"; (b) "My love life does not represent me. It is one of the many projects that I will participate in during my lifetime. I'd best not judge myself by any one of them or I will put my emotions at the mercy of my successes or failures"; (c) "Self-evaluation is immoral in that it leads to hurting myself: If I estimate myself to have more worth when my love life is going strong, I will judge myself to be bad when my love life could or begins to falter."
FF: Emotional relief, peacefulness, clearheadedness.
GC: Love-life problems are often problems of self-evaluation. Giving yourself a report card with a high mark when able to gain favorable love experiences leads to giving yourself that same report card with a low mark when experiencing less-than-hoped-for love advantages. Emotional flip-flopping can be set aside by strongly understanding that you are not your love life and that having love doesn't make you superhuman any more than not having it makes you subhuman. Self-judgments will throw cold water on even the best of love relationships. You will likely worry about losing what you have made the sacred estimate of your life, fearfully blundering on in attempting to retain this essential factor.

3. IB: *Love is both natural and naturally easy.*
FSS: "Because love is such a natural thing I shouldn't have to work very hard to maintain it - if I fall into love I should fall into happiness."
IE: Complacency, listlessness, lethargy, inertia.
CSS: (a) "I'd best see that although falling in love is like falling off a log, maintaining it is more like sawing a log: The only thing that works is working"; (b) "Although I can easily attach myself to a love partner, I had better work hard at maintaining that attachment"; (c) "Little comes easy but trouble, and that's exactly what I'm likely to give myself unless I accept that love's inspiration is often a companion of persistent perspiration."

FF: Alertness, vigor, motivation.

GC: People often have problems in their love relationships not so much because they change, but because they stubbornly refuse to change. Refusing to give up the impossible dream of eternal bliss served on a silver platter leads to a childish refusal to put oneself through the toil that is often required to keep a good thing going well.

4. IB: *Love and agreement, compatibility, and/or obligation are sacredly linked and therefore by necessity go together.*

FSS: "Those who love me are required to always agree with, support, and console me and oblige my every request and desire. I in turn must make like provisions for them. If by chance either of us falters in these statutory commitments, it is to be viewed as a breach of loyalty and means one loves the other less."

IE: Guilt by the violator; betrayal and anger by the receiver.

CSS: (a) "In many ways it is better when my partner and I are in sync with our opinions and wishes. However, because we are not clones of one another it is natural that this will not always be the case"; (b) "Not believing ourselves to be servants of one another's wishes will make for a relationship based on choice rather than compulsion. Such loosening up of duty-bound beliefs will afford us less dependency and more carefreeness"; (c) "By agreeing to disagree we can learn much from one another in our different opinions."

FF: Tolerance, acceptance, grace, forgiveness.

GC: Love does not conquer all, and it is not the answer to everything - including incompatibility. People are different, and to think that these differences violate love ties invites emotional fallout. Uniting varying tastes can be like trying to fit round pegs into square holes. Although better accommodating individual differences is preferable it cannot always be done. Couples would do well to stay away from the notion "Agree with what I have to say or you don't love me." Relationships that do not stand the test of controversy probably won't stand the test of time.

5. IB: *Love must be reciprocal, and when it is not the other is to be condemned and punished as a rotten person.*
   FSS: "If I take the time and energy to attach myself to someone else, especially if I go out of my way to treat him with no lapses in kindness and consideration, he is required to give me a return on my investment. If he does not return the favor, I'll hate his guts until the day he dies - and I hope it's soon."
   IE: Betrayal, anger, hurt, hostility.
   CSS: (a) "Others have free will - not my will. My choice is whether to bond with them. Their choice is whether to return the bonding. They may make what I view to be a bad choice, but that does not make them bad"; (b) "People have a right to select and discriminate against me as much as I have a right to make myself biased toward them"; (c) "Attaching myself to someone else is not to be taken lightly. However, because I put forth the effort to connect emotionally with them does not mean they are required to do the same."
   FF: Keen but healthy disappointment, regret, sadness.
   GC: Many people fall in love as a childish excuse to insist on reciprocation. The invented reverse golden rule of "others have to do unto me as I do unto them" had best be uninvented. The fact that someone is on a different wavelength as you does not constitute a federal crime and does not qualify him or her for the scum bucket.

6. IB: *Love has the power to destroy you.*
   FSS: "I'm at the emotional mercy of the status of my love life. When I extend my love efforts my life is controlled/determined by that status. Because I am at the mercy of my love experiences, they are to be feared and approached with extreme caution."
   IE: Anxiety, fear, stress, tension.

CSS: (a) "Although it is doubtful I would be unflappable in the throes of love disappointments, I would not have to do an emotional tilt in the event of such disenchantment"; (b) "I'm not a trained seal, rat, or guinea pig. Thus, I can think for myself in ways that can allow me not to turn sadness into tragedy"; (c) "Negative results in my love life can only dissatisfy and frustrate me; only by exaggerating the significance of these can I make myself disturbed."
FF: Healthy concern, apprehension, confidence.
GC: Events do not cause emotions. Beliefs about those events do. Emotions verify what you believe about a circumstance. Curtailing overreactive thoughts by viewing matters in deliberate and not desperate ways permits you to override, rather than be overridden by, love's happenings. Your emotions do not represent your love life but rather your beliefs about your love life.

7. IB: *Love means getting yourself upset about your loved one's problems and disturbances.*
FSS: "If my partner is upset I have to get myself at least equally upset. If I don't that means I love her less and that is a breach of my undying loyalty to the relationship. In addition, for not putting myself in a similar bad emotional way, I'm a bad partner and/or person."
IE: Guilt, depression.
CSS: (a) "My level of upset about my partner's concerns has nothing to do with the price of tamales as far as my love for her. In fact, not taking her as seriously as she is taking herself may be an act of love in itself"; (b) "Part of love is trying to be helpful in the time of your partner's adversity. The less upset I make myself, the more clearheadedly helpful I will likely be."
FF: Composure, deliberation.
GC: Upsetting oneself and then having two people upset about the same thing is not the loving, helpful thing to do. Getting rid of this narrow equation - more upset = more caring - helps moderate the

amount of feeling that is against the relationship's best interest.

8. IB: *The only alternative to love is loneliness, and therefore lack of love has to lead to despair.*
   FSS: "Being without love means being without anything and everything. If I'm alone there is nothing I can do to prevent loneliness and distress from setting in. When love's gone - I'm a goner."
   IE: Depression, worry, anxiety.
   CSS: "Being without someone doesn't mean being without anything. In fact, if I play my cards right I can take advantage of the increased freedom and choices of going solo. My being alone will not lead to any place in particular other than where I direct it."
   FF: Anticipation, challenge, excitement.
   GC: Being alone is often turned into the self-fulfilling promise of loneliness. Much can be experienced and learned from solitude if favorable options are not blocked by deterministic thinking.

9. IB: *Overcoming fear of losing in love can be done by withdrawing from involvements.*
   FSS: "If I try to gain mutual love I'm afraid I might fail. For me to get over this fear it is best that I avoid all appearances of what I am afraid of because then it will go away by itself."
   IE: Worry, fear, anxiety, desperation.
   CSS: (a) "By consistently taking my fears with me and exposing myself to the possibility of losing the love I am afraid of losing, I will likely develop an immunity to my fears"; (b) "A good way to overcome my fear of losing out in love is to convince myself of the truth - that such an occurrence would be bearable rather than terrible, horrible, and catastrophic"; (c) "I won't learn how to swim by knowing that I am required to get into the water and move my arms; it would be best if I actually did it. So too, I won't learn love-seeking skills by just thinking about them - I would do better to develop a philosophy of actual participation and nonavoidance."

FF: Anticipation, confidence, deliberation.
GC: Purposeful, fearful avoidance of an activity often makes it appear bigger than life. Making contact with the same happening (especially repeatedly) brings it clearer into focus as a part of life. The further you go into the mouth of the dragon, the less you are likely to fear the dragon.

10. IB: *Love is a 50-50 proposition.*
FSS: "My partner should do his half of the relationship work, and I should do mine. This will result in us living happily ever after. If by chance our tabulations don't turn out to be 'Even Stephen' it can only be interpreted as one maliciously taking advantage of the other."
IE: Betrayal, self-pity, resentment.
CSS: (a) "It is nice when my partner and I both work together on our relationship, but it is not necessary that we keep score of our efforts"; (b) "For us to be in never-ending sync we would have to be perfect. Perfectionism is not a human trait; it would be wise to expect and accept our faults"; (c) "Relationships are more like 60-40, 30-70, or 80-20 depending on the daily effort of each partner - it would be best for me to allow for this range of human variability and inequality."
FF: Appropriate annoyance and disappointment, forgiveness.
GC: A certain amount of reasonable inequality had best be accepted in any relationship. To try to perfectly fine-tune a relationship can only multiply existing frustrations.

11. IB: *Love is more trouble than it's worth.*
FSS: "Gaining and maintaining a love relationship is such a hassle, I'll take on an attitude of 'I don't care, what's the difference?' It's just too strenuous to get into the act of love so I'll just sit on the sidelines and pretend it doesn't matter."
IE: Casualness, listlessness, lethargy, inertia.

CSS: (a) "Like any project worth its salt, love requires lots of energy. Sometimes such effort will pay off, sometimes it won't. However, meaning can be gained by trying, which can take on a life of its own. Succeeding, which would be frosting on the cake, is always an additional worthwhile possibility"; (b) "Like most humans, I have a strong preference for closeness and affection. Finding such experiences at times may seem futile. However, why not go for more of the marbles and put my efforts into what I prize at a higher level rather than toward a lesser value? What better way to spend my time than to actively seek out what is important to me"; (c) "Taking a flippant, casual view toward what I value in life is not going to intensify my existence."

FF: Motivation, vital absorption, increased energy.

GC: Acting like something really doesn't matter when it really does often disguises a fear of failure and anguish about the pain that one will be required to put oneself through to accomplish a goal. Some comfort can be found in a laid-back mentality that camouflages failure and discomfort anxieties.

12. IB: *Past failure experiences in love must have a strong influence on how you continue to love, indefinitely.*

FSS: "Because I have previously floundered in my love relationships I will continue to falter, because the past sets the groundwork for the present and future."

IE: Resignation, depression, lethargy, hopelessness.

CSS: (a) "I can learn from my past failures rather than repeat them"; (b) "The past is a bridge to the present, but it does not determine the present or future"; (c) "It is just as important to learn what doesn't work in building love relationships as it is to discover what does; my failures have taught me just that."

FF: Hope, anticipation, courage, inspiration.

GC: Failing has advantages when you play your cards right. Putting what you've learned from your flaws in the past to good use can help you to succeed in present relationships. To believe that the past is the master of your future makes for an uninspired viewpoint on love with a mind closed to more favorable outcomes.

13. IB: *Without love you have nothing at all.*
    FSS: "Love is everything; without it I could not find any value to myself or discover any enjoyment in life."
    IE: Fear, worry, anxiety, panic, depression.
    CSS: (a) "Love is one of the better if not near the best things I could have going for myself. However, as big a part of my life as it might be, it is not bigger than my life"; (b) "If one part of my life (such as love) wavers, it does not mean that the rest is required to extinguish"; (c) "With love I have one set of advantages; without love I have a different range of advantages. It would be best for me to focus on those dimensions that I have going for me at the present moment in my life."
    FF: Appreciation, happiness, joy.
    GC: Commercialized views of love would like you to believe that love is the alpha and omega to a satisfying existence. Using all-or-nothing thinking to make sacred the value love has for you will likely be emotionally disruptive for your love-seeking purposes.

14. IB: *Human beings have an unlimited capacity to give and receive love.*
    FSS: "I should be able to provide, and others should be able to supply me, an unlimited supply of love. If either of us falters in achieving our fullest potential we are to be condemned for not placing among the very loving."
    IE: Guilt, anxiety, depression.
    CSS: (a) "I'd best give myself the benefit of the doubt and have a decent respect for, though not an intimidation of, human limitations. I am limited in whatever I do - including my ability to give and receive provisions of love"; (b) "It is regretful when I find myself not being able to provide or receive the

amount of love I would like. However, this deficiency does not constitute a calamity"; (c) "If I don't put so much pressure on myself I may well be able to lighten up while opening up my availability to send and receive love."

FF: Peacefulness, clearheadedness, acceptance.

GC: Love is not at the fingertips of all who wish to create and experience it. Love is a very desirable experience for most. As soon as we insist that we have to experience what is favorable we lose sight of our limited potential, put undue pressure on ourself to do what we can only allow - not force - ourself to do, and block ourself from letting what capacity we do have show through.

15. IB: *Love relationships should not have conditions attached to them.*

FSS: "If I really love someone there will be no conditions attached to our relationship. If I do impose conditions this means (a) I love the other less, and (b) I'm being selfish. True love means giving until it hurts and then giving some more with no expectation in return."

IE: False hopes, ultimate betrayal and self pity, guilt.

CSS: (a) "Because I wish some profit and advantage from my love relationships means I care enough about them to gain from them so I can then more conveniently give to them"; (b) "By defining my wants I encourage give-and-take and discourage the attitude of taking for granted, resulting in a variety of experiences for both of us - and variety is one of the spices of love"; (c) "By getting my partner to respond to me instead of one-sidedly responding to her I am encouraging rotation and balance in the everyday interactions out of which mutually satisfying relationships are carved"; (d) "By increasing my leverage and bargaining power I will likely put myself in a better position to gain in my love life. I can then reinvest this profit for the benefit of both of us."

FF: Security, confidence, realistic optimism.

GC: Far from being selfish, expecting provisions from your partner is of benefit to your partner, you, and the relationship. It is fair to your partner because he or she now knows what is important for you and doesn't have to guess as to how to warm the cockles of your heart. Once he or she meets your expectations he or she will have the added benefit of finding you more fun to be around. It is to your advantage to be the recipient of your partner's desirable conduct. The relationship itself is likely to pay dividends from your favorable social exchange agreements and follow-through.

16. IB: *Love conquers all.*
FSS: "Love is like my guardian angel - everything will be all right because of it."
IE: False hopes, complacency, lethargy.
CSS: (a) "Love is important, but it will not move mountains nor perform major surgery on individual differences with my partner"; (b) "Love is not a magical potion. It is not to be viewed as a substitute for the hard work necessary to carve out compromises on matters of mutual concern"; (c) "Falling into love is not the same as falling into happiness. The latter is to be worked out, worked on, and worked at rather than be seen as happening automatically."
FF: Incentive, realistic anticipation and participation.
GC: Humans tend to direct themselves toward what appears easier. Commercialized views of love make it convenient to view eternal happiness as an automatic companion to love. Love sustained comes from the ingenuity and hard work necessary to make yourself hard to resist. Love as a never-ending conqueror overlooks this grim - but not too grim - reality.

17. IB: *If after much frustration you decide to stop loving someone, you're a failure.*
FSS: "I've put so much into this relationship and I've gotten nearly nothing in return, but if I fail to com-

plete what I started I'd be a failure and couldn't live with or by myself."
IE: Insecurity, fear, guilt.
CSS: (a) "Finally realizing that it's time to stop trying to revive a dead relationship is something to rejoice about rather than put myself down about"; (b) "I can do myself a favor by dropping the ball if the ball game has long been over"; (c) "Everybody makes mistakes but I don't have to continue to make mine."
FF: Surety, confidence, emotional relief.
GC: Taking a bad situation and not making it worse - not duplicating a mistake - stems from admitting your poor judgment to begin with combined with the resolve to start over. Seeing that your original failure does not represent you permits movement in a more promising direction.

18. IB: *Love increases sexual arousal.*
FSS: "Because love and sex are so natural they should come together naturally easy. Love equals sex; therefore, if one is good, the other should be, too. Romantic love makes for romantic sex - no way should I be required to inconvenience myself to enjoy sex - rather than do that I'll roll over and go to sleep."
IE: Resentment, high frustration, complacency, lethargy.
CSS: (a) "If I wish to heighten my sexual arousal I'd best do what would be compatible with that goal - focus on my physiology and special sexy thoughts - after the sex I can focus on how much I love my partner"; (b) In sex, or any other worthwhile endeavor, little works but working"; (c) "In many ways love is incompatible with and a distraction to sex; if I don't keep my mind on what is sexy for me, how can I expect to achieve sexual ends?"
FF: Motivation, incentive, anticipation, acceptance.
GC: Although it is more convenient to believe that love will naturally increase sexual arousal with little energy output it does not stand the test of a law of learning. If you are going to accomplish a goal you are likely to be required to vigorously focus on the

substance of your objective rather than sidetrack yourself. If you are eating a gourmet meal and you focus on how much you love the cook rather than relishing each morsel of the food he or she has prepared you will likely enjoy the meal less. Likewise, if you focus on loving thoughts, your sexual appetite will likely diminish.

19. IB: *Love means always understanding (without explanation or request).*
FSS: "After all this time if my partner really loved me he would know what I want without me having to ask."
IE: Resentment, self-pity, anger.
CSS: (a) "If my partner were a mind reader he would have gotten rich on the stock market by now"; (b) "Where is it written that my partner has to draw me out, baby me, pamper me, or in any other manner, shape, or form read my bloody mind"; (c) "Am I helpless or so lazy that I can't let my wants be known without wrongly thinking that my partner is supposed to do my work for me?"
FF: Self-initiative, motivation.
GC: Mates have enough of their own desires to monitor without being expected to stay one step ahead of yours. This irrational belief is rooted in the childish insistence upon unending protection and being taken care of.

20. IB: *Love means always saying yes.*
FSS: "If you really love me you will always cater to my wishes and never say no."
IE: Resentment, anger, self-pity, hurt.
CSS: (a) "Others have free will, not my will"; (b) "Because I like to be accommodated by my partner does not mean that she is obliged to do so"; (c) "There is no evidence that what is important to my partner as it contrasts to what is important to me has anything to do with her love for me."
FF: Patience, tolerance, acceptance.

GC: The tendency to take someone's refusal of a request personally accounts for the hurt that follows such a turning away. This insistent irrational idea that love means that under all conditions you must not deny my request, attempts to perfume such potential discomfort.

21. IB: *If you love someone you don't use him.*
FSS: "If he really loved me he wouldn't expect advantages, conveniences, or favors from me."
IE: Resentment, bitterness, despisement.
CSS: (a) "Why is it so unusual for people to search for profit, gain, and advantage from those they love"; (b) "Expecting profits from a love relationship keeps interest high, discourages taking the relationship for granted, and encourages give-and-take"; (c) "It is nice to give *and* receive; why must my partner not have a strong preference for both?"
FF: Understanding, caring, acceptance.
GC: The very reason we permit ourselves to fall in love is to use what provisions our partner affords. Love is a convenience item - it is convenient to fall in love with someone when they please us by the assets they provide for our use (e.g., looks, intelligence, creativity, humor, etc.). If partners didn't expect such provisions from one another there would be less motivation to make themselves harder to resist by putting their best foot forward.

22. IB: *My partner has to admit she is wrong and change before I can be happy.*
FSS: "My mate makes me upset and therefore is responsible for my feelings. She must admit what she is doing to me so that I can then live happily ever after."
IE: Anger, hostility, resentment.
CSS: (a) "Nobody has ever invented a way to change somebody else - I'd best put my money down on: 'My, how you have changed since I have changed' "; (b) "Because one part of my life is not going well does not mean that the rest has to go down the tubes";

(c) "If I'm not accountable and responsible for my own problems, who is? Better that I not put my personal happiness at the mercy of someone else's conduct lest I live my life on an emotional shoestring."
FF: Self-reliance, tolerance, self-confidence, clear-headedness.
GC: Happiness is not externally caused. You don't have to make yourself dependent on circumstances and people to change before you can begin to experience more of the joys and less of the hassles of life.

23. IB: *Love means always telling others what they want to hear.*
FSS: "I am responsible for my partner's feelings. Therefore, I should only say things that I know he is going to take kindly to. Besides, I can't stand it when he voices his upset.
IE: High stress, fear, guilt, other-pity.
CSS: (a) "If I can't make my partner happy I can't make him miserable either"; (b) "By assuming my mate would be an emotional cripple in the face of my honest opinion I am not giving him my confidence nor encouraging him to develop to his fuller emotional potential"; (c) "Not rocking the boat can sometimes lead to the kind of peace found in graveyards. If our love cannot tolerate the test of disagreement, perhaps we'd best look at its weak links more closely."
FF: Goodwill, other-confidence, less stress and strain.
GC: Being honest - under the umbrella of saying what the other wants to hear - is not likely to be the substance of which long-term relationships are made. Some degree of open, honest, level-headed discussions are helpful if couples more fully wish to get to know and trust one another.

24. IB: *Love means always being totally honest.*
FSS: "No matter what the potential consequences I must always be totally honest with my partner; if I should intentionally or unintentionally slip this would mean that I love her less."

IE: Anxiety, guilt.
CSS: (a) "I'd do well to distinguish between a white lie and a black truth. Just as I would not give my mate a food she was allergic to, I would think twice about saying something that she would predictably overreact to"; (b) "Show me a relationship where a certain amount of catering doesn't go on, and I'll show you a relationship that's made in heaven - and I know of no relationships that are made in heaven"; (c) "Respecting another's unfortunate sore spots enough to tip-toe around them can be a loving thing to do."
FF: Respect, tolerance, forgiveness.
GC: There are exceptions to practically every rule. Because a trait such as honesty is preferable does not mean that it has to be compulsively applied. Like anything else, use it only when it is to the long-range advantage of you and your love life.

25. IB: *When two people love each other there is invariably a right, precise, perfect solution to each of their problems and it is catastrophic when this is not found.*
FSS: "Well-intended love will take care of problems, regardless of whether it is backed by the right methods. How humongously awful it would be if this did not turn out to be the case."
IE: High frustration, guilt, heightened anguish.
CSS: (a) "Why is it so strange, and why do I have to make myself feel so disheartened, when we can't unlock the secret to all our problems and concerns"; (b) "Is it really sacred and all-important that we find all the solutions to our problems? Can we not simply agree to disagree - with no love lost in the process"; (c) "Face it - love is not the answer to everything - and sometimes not to anything!"
FF: Acceptance, tolerance, emotional relief.
GC: Because people are different they are likely to have boundary disputes. Negotiating compromises about these differences rather than lamenting the fact that they exist would seem like a better route to go.
26. IB: *To trust a loved one (especially if he or she has once betrayed your trust) is dangerous and fearsome;*

therefore you should be terribly concerned about it and keep dwelling on the worst possibility recurring.
FSS: "Betrayal is catastrophic. If I worry about it enough my concerns will show and prevent such an awesome event."
IE: Worry, fear, high stress.
CSS: (a) "Trusting myself enough to be able to stand on my own two feet in the event I would lose my mate makes it more convenient for me to trust him"; (b) "There is no magic; thinking does not make it so. In fact, the more I fool myself into thinking I can use worry to head off what I foolishly believe would be disaster, the more likely I will assist in producing the results I wish to avoid"; (c) "If I lose him - he loses me!"
FF: Self-confidence, emotional independence, emotional relief.
GC: Mistrust of another is often rooted in insecurity, a mistrust of self. Minimizing fears of abandonment by trusting one's own emotional sustaining potential permits a more refreshing, concerned but not consumed perspective on the relationship.

Emotional dependency is not like a virus. It is neither caught from someone else nor cured by someone else. Some things cannot be done to or for another person. Tying and untying dependency knots is one of those items. Try to distinguish between love and dependency. Love is energizing, increases vitality, is in your best experiential interest, and allows you to let go when you sense the relationship is over. Dependency exhausts, drains, and saps you, and works against your best emotional interests. If you find you have put yourself in such an emotional straitjacket, decide to become your own physician and heal yourself from the faulty notions that you bind yourself with. Untie and unblock yourself from your rigid rules of loving, perhaps not helping yourself to ultimate emotional freedom - but certainly to making yourself to be easier and more enjoying in the relationship.

The "Prophet" Motive: Predicting the Future as It Profits Your Mental Health

"It's easy to make myself angry, to watch television rather than complete a project, to push myself off a diet, to continue to smoke, and to avoid conflict that often goes along with holding to your opinion." If you believe the idea implied in some of these examples - that it's easy to take the easy way out - perhaps you can profit from the prophet motive as it pays interest and dividends to your long-range happiness and survival. This guide presents a more enduring perspective that extends beyond the pleasure of the moment and services the idea of not necessarily feeling better right now, but better for the rest of your life.

Mental health is to think, feel, and act in a way that is in your best interest and includes the ability to predict the future. Mental health is to convince yourself that what you decide today will affect your tomorrows; that there is a piper to pay, and that the future will pay its dues and come home to roost. You can shoot your wad today and have a hangover tomorrow or exercise restraint today and feel better tomorrow. Overcoming the all-too-frequent human tendency to reduce motivation to immediate comfort and convenience requires a vision of better long-range consequences that are an outcome of accepting temporary inconveniences.

Shortsightedness is a handicap that results in long-term advantages being put on the back burner. Immediate pleasure is acknowledged while long-term negative consequences are pushed out of mind. The pleasure of the moment is dramatized and long-range pain goes unrecognized. In the mind's eye, short-range comforts dominate long-term discontent. Instead of installing short-run sacrifices for long-range gain, future gain is exchanged for present pleasure.

To install your crystal ball and exercise mind over platter, matter, or chatter, work at using the following methods that will encourage a long-range view of life.

1. *Powerful self-motivational coping ideas:*

   - "The line of least resistance is often the line of most resistance."
   - "Nothing works but working."
   - "It's not easy to take the easy way out."
   - "Doing gets it done."
   - "Start by starting."
   - "Present pain for future gain."
   - "Little gain without pain."
   - "Hard as it is to do, it's harder not to."
   - "Short-run sacrifice is a small price to pay for long-range gains."
   - "Do I want to feel better now or better for the rest of my life?"
   - "People who run from pain are likely to suffer more pain; those who face pain are likely to suffer less."
   - "Little comes easy but trouble and calories."
   - "The first step is the hardest."
   - "I can stand what I don't like."
   - "Get behind yourself and push."
   - "Do it as if you felt like doing it."
   - "Inspiration comes from perspiration."
   - "If I'm waiting for something to turn up I'd best start with my sleeves."
   - "Forget 'yes, but' and get off your butt."
   - "Doing decisions are better than talking decisions."
   - "Walk the walk rather than talk the talk."
   - "Don't wait for the tomorrows that may never come."

- "Put one foot in front of the other."
- "What am I asking myself to do that hasn't been done before?"
- "Practice is the best of teachers."
- "Doing the best I can may prepare me to be lucky."

There you have it, 26 examples of motivational self-statements. Highlight those that would be especially helpful for you. Piggyback on these with some of your own. Then, transpose the more helpful one-liners onto a note card and carry them with you. Last, practice *forcefully* stating them to yourself, preferably out loud, several times a day. Get your own motivational attention by your active, avid recitations of these simple ideas for increasing incentive. Get so you can state these to yourself as naturally as you can recollect your middle initial or telephone number. Use these spontaneous self-statements to interrupt putting off until tomorrow what you have already put off until today. Then: . . . .

2. *Vividly call to mind long-range advantages.* In lieu of overfocusing on the immediate discomfort of getting started today, tabulate the long-range pleasures of tomorrow's completion. Pool your imagery resources in a way that displays your after-the-effort prophecies in technicolor. Such long-range emphasis will encourage the type of sustained effort required to round off rather than go around your goals. Write these long-term advantages on a note card and review them daily, each time strongly renewing your appreciation for tomorrow's advantages.
3. *Cultivate a philosophy of challenge.* Humans would rather shirk than work. Expect yourself to be one of the few who consistently get behind themselves and push. Keenly appreciate the heavy doses of meaning and satisfaction that come from expecting yourself to put one foot in front of the other en route to reaching your goals.
4. *Carve out an attitude of nonavoidance.* Make up your mind to wear out rather than rust out in making contact with problems and concerns. Strenuously and forcefully prod yourself toward meeting the requirements of long-term accomplishment.

5. *Penalize lack of effort.* Agree on ways to get your own attention if you do not follow through with task expectations by a certain time. Contract with yourself to monitor and manage your behavior by giving yourself a self-imposed penalty for stalling beyond the designated boundary. Such penalties as the immediate pain of getting up 2 hours earlier for the next month, eating your least favorite foods for 2 days, or burning a $20 bill can be avoided by fulfilling the requirements of long-range pleasure. If you don't follow through with the self-assigned penalty perhaps this is a tip-off that you're not serious about becoming an active prophet of your own well-being.
6. *Tell others.* Explaining to others the nuts and bolts of what you wish to accomplish, how you intend to do so, and the rational advantages anticipated at project's end is another dimension to soliciting your own incentive.
7. *Prepare to pay the entry fee.* The first self-propelled push is often the most difficult. Part of self-regulated motivation is the acceptance of this immediate reality. See that once you get yourself in gear you will likely naturally build upon your motion. Humans tend to go in the direction they are headed - once they get themselves in gear.
8. *Strongly despise your actions or inactions without despising yourself.* By vigorously putting down your procrastinating tendencies you will be better able to keep their negative impact on your life fresh in mind. This view may encourage you to avoid such negative consequences. Taking yourself a step beyond such strong contemplations to self-condemnation will likely choke off the clearheaded planning required to make fewer mistakes in the future.
9. *Don't insist on guarantees.* Perfectionistically requiring a long-term pay-off for your immediate efforts when there is no such assurance is not conducive to putting out the amount of energy required to increase the chances of eventual profit. The gold-plated guarantee requested becomes tarnished in the face of the realities of uncertainty in an uncertain world.

10. *Avoid comfort trappings.* Little is gained without pain. Don't shortsightedly trap yourself with the idea that you're in the world to feel comfortable and that any experience short of that is to be avoided like the plague. Instead of startling and intimidating yourself by discomfort, accept the idea that you're in the world to experience the world - and that includes a fair amount of discomfort, especially of the short-run variety.
11. *Get rid of the ego.* Don't put yourself on the line. Don't use long-run potential profits for esteem-building purposes. If you use a self-esteem model that calculates your worth in proportion to your profit or deficit margins you will likely skirt all appearances of potential failure. Avoid trapping yourself from your ego-building definitions. Destroy the ego by uprooting self-fulfilling prophecies that lead to self-downing and emotional upset. True, if you try in the present you might fail in the future. But it's not true that your failures would make you "unworthier than all" any more than success would bring you to "holier than thou."
12. *Heighten your emotional threshold.* Train yourself to endure frustration by using the coping ideas reviewed in point number one. Accept that just as it takes repetitions to build physical muscle, so too is repetition the mother of learning in developing emotional muscle. Repeatedly think in terms of taking long-range views of life. Regularly make contact with those circumstances and projects that would support the idea of getting on with your life in ways that help you to not just feel better today - but get better over the course of a lifetime.

What does it profit a person if he or she loses his or her short-range discomfort only to suffer more over the long haul? Why not seek out the long-run dividends that accrue from enlightened prophecies that put your money down on eventual gains? What is the real gain of immediately experiencing the comforts of the world only to lose greater long-run comforts? Making short-run sacrifices for long-run gains is both an art and a science. Examining the evidence behind the question "Is it wiser to feel better now or better for the rest of my life?" provides scientific validity to your choices. Waiting for something to turn up while starting with your sleeves will unleash your natural, artistic, problem-solving potential. Why not paint a life picture that has you giving yourself fuller consideration to your eventual interests?

ADDENDUMS

Addendum 1

Self-Instructional Coping Statements

1. I'd best not judge myself by my behavior.
2. Others' opinions do not equal me.
3. Asking impossible questions such as asking for tomorrow's answers today only creates confusion.
4. Others' rejection of me does not make me inferior or diminish me in any way.
5. Life does not have to be perfect.
6. I do not have to be perfect.
7. I have a right to be wrong.
8. I have a right to fail.
9. Others have a right to be wrong.
10. Others have a right to fail.
11. Others don't have to act the way I want them to - after all, I don't run the universe.
12. Life does not have to be easy, and I don't have to make it so when it isn't.
13. Others do not have to treat me kindly.
14. Life isn't fair; there is no reason why it has to be.
15. It is not awful when things go wrong.
16. People and events don't have to be the way I want them to be.
17. I don't have to have my own way.
18. It is best for me not to act so demandingly.
19. Because something would be nice does not mean it is necessary.
20. I don't have to get what I think I deserve.

21. Because something is good does not mean I have to have it.
22. I don't have to have my own way, or whine when I don't get it.
23. Because something is hard does not mean it is too hard.
24. Because something is unpleasant does not mean it shouldn't be.
25. Because something is unpleasant does not mean I can't stand it.
26. I am not bad for acting badly.
27. I'd best focus on what I am doing and not how well I am doing or what other people might be thinking.
28. I can accept my feelings rather than make myself afraid of them.
29. I don't have to know tomorrow's answers today.
30. Making the right decision is important but not all-important.
31. I will survive and won't be diminished as a human being because of someone else's lack of approval of me.
32. Failure isn't the worst of all possible crimes.
33. Cool it/slow down/go easy/give yourself some slack.
34. I don't have to have all or even any particular advantage that life has to offer.
35. Many things are a part of life, but nothing is bigger than life.
36. Adversity is not the end of the world.
37. I am not responsible for finding solutions to other people's problems and disturbances.
38. I can stand what I don't like.
39. Being true to myself is more important to me than others' approval.
40. Others' approval is nice - but not necessary.
41. I can't make other people happy.
42. Think it through first.
43. Disappointments are not disasters.
44. Love and approval are very definitely nice, but my life does not depend upon them.
45. Possibilities are not probabilities or inevitabilities.
46. I am responsible for how I feel, not others or circumstances - others don't give me feelings nor do I give others feelings.
47. Nothing is more than bad or awful.
48. Tough beans (when things don't work out)!
49. The past doesn't get any better.
50. Life doesn't have to be fair or single me out for any special favors, and I don't have to bemoan my plight and feel sorry for myself when it doesn't.
51. I can be myself, I don't have to prove myself.
52. Others don't give me feelings, I create my own.

53. Doing things well is satisfying and usually brings advantages, but it is human to make mistakes.
54. I can forgive myself for acting badly.
55. I can correct my mistakes without condemning myself.
56. I am not a louse for acting lousily.
57. I can't make other people upset or give them feelings in any way.
58. I have free will, my feelings aren't determined.
59. Feeling anxious, nervous, or depressed is part of being human.
60. Doing gets it done.
61. Nothing seems to work but working.
62. Inspiration comes from perspiration.
63. It is to my advantage to do it now, not later.
64. Short-range sacrifices can lead to long-range advantages.
65. I can forgive myself for making mistakes.
66. I can forgive others for being wrong.
67. I can wonder without worrying.
68. Important doesn't mean urgent.
69. Nothing is bigger than life.
70. Sad doesn't mean tragic.
71. There is no such thing as a perfect time to do what is best.
72. When I get myself angry, I only repeat the other person's mistakes.
73. It is impossible to get angry without hurting myself.
74. Do it whether you feel like it or not.
75. Because I haven't done something up until now doesn't mean I can't ever do it.
76. Anything worth doing is worth doing poorly.
77. It is better to do than to do well.
78. Trying to do well doesn't mean doing perfectly well.
79. The past is not the present or future.
80. I don't have to get a fair return from my efforts.
81. There is nothing under the sun to feel shame about.
82. I don't have to blame myself for my faults.
83. The past is a bridge to the present.
84. I'd best be concerned without being consumed.
85. Important doesn't mean urgent.
86. Don't mountain climb over molehills.
87. Important doesn't mean all-important.
88. Someone liking or loving me is not a life-or-death matter.
89. Because someone says something doesn't make it so.
90. There is more than one way of looking at things.
91. Don't put off until tomorrow what you have already put off until today.

92. Be yourself, don't prove yourself.
93. I'd better stop challenging what I can't change.
94. I don't avoid failure by not trying.
95. I can always have value to myself.
96. I'd better accept that I get what I get and not what I deserve.
97. I wouldn't want to get what I deserve all the time.
98. It is not what happens to me that is most important but what I do with what happens to me.
99. Because something is good doesn't mean that I have to have it.
100. Because something is bad does not mean that it is not tolerable or must not exist.
101. Others have free will and can trespass on my values if they choose.
102. I have free will and can draw my own conclusions and make my own choices apart from what others might think.
103. Perfection paralyzes and I'm not perfect!!
104. I can't change what has already happened so I'd best accept it.
105. I don't have to buckle under.
106. I don't have to make a federal case out of it.
107. Having disadvantages in life doesn't diminish my value to myself as a human being.
108. I'd best accept that I get what I get in life and not what I deserve.
109. Would I always want to get what I deserve?
110. Others' advantages don't make them loftier human beings.
111. Because I failed doesn't mean I have to continue to fail.
112. Being alone doesn't mean I have to be lonely.
113. I don't have to blame myself for my faults.
114. Being guilty doesn't mean I have to feel guilty.
115. I am accountable for my mistakes but not blameworthy because of them.
116. Perfectionism is the pursuit of *un*happiness.
117. Making short-run sacrifices for long-run gains is important and rewarding.
118. Working on my problems is worth the effort.
119. Knowledge isn't the same as action.
120. Knowing something and convincing myself of something are two different things.
121. It is not true that because it took a long time to create my problems it is going to take a long time to solve them.
122. Simple doesn't mean easy or simply lived.
123. Make doing decisions not just talking decisions.
124. Life is sometimes a hassle, but not a horror.
125. People don't give me feelings, I create my own.

126. Take a long-range and not a short-range view of life.
127. It's best that I accept present pain for future gain.
128. I can stand anything - including temptation.
129. Involvement yes, entanglement no!
130. It's not what I know, it's what I do with what I know.
131. I can be adventuresome without being foolhardy.
132. Preferable is not mandatory or essential.
133. Deliberation is different from desperation.
134. It is not easy to take the easy way out.
135. Sharing my life with others is good, sacrificing my life for others isn't.
136. Acceptance is a major change.
137. Don't amplify, multiply, inflate, magnify, escalate, blow-up, or pyramid unwanted or unpleasant circumstances and feelings.
138. Self-correction, yes! Self-condemnation, no!
139. I can consider matters without brooding about them.
140. Conscientiousness doesn't mean perfectionism.
141. I can prioritize things without dramatizing them.
142. Desire and demand are two different things.
143. I don't have to throw gasoline on my concerns.
144. Less than ideal doesn't mean awful.
145. A slip does not mean a major setback.
146. All is not lost if I do the wrong thing, only if I keep doing the wrong things.
147. Wondering about life means I have interest in it; worrying about it will result in losing that same interest.
148. It's best that I be more interested in controlling myself than in trying to control others.
149. When I win an argument or a fight, I lose.
150. I don't have to feel anxious or afraid when I don't know what to expect.
151. Caring less can be helpful, but doesn't mean uncaring.
152. I don't create conditions of life but I do create my response toward these conditions.
153. Nothing in life *has* to be.
154. Lighten up, but don't give up.

Addendum 2

Expanded Nutritional Self-Statements

1. It is not necessary to have certainty before arriving at a decision. Once a decision is made it can be lived with. To hesitate, stumble around, and second-guess possible outcomes only wastes time and creates unnecessary burdens. Think! Make a decision! Manage the outcome!
2. Put forth strong effort. If that's not good enough - too bad - but not shameful, horrible, embarrassing, or the end of the world. Even if I didn't put forth strong effort, I still wouldn't be required to down myself or make myself feel ashamed.
3. When in a group or audience, concentrate on what you are doing, not how well you are doing or what other people might be thinking. To not do so only causes paralysis of the analysis with its handicapping self-consciousness.
4. Not doing as well as I would like only proves that I am human and is only a source of disturbance if I make it so. I refuse to beat myself over my head with my shortcomings and mistakes.
5. I need not upset myself with real or imaginary negative thoughts and opinions that others have or may have of me or my actions.
6. When something appears fearsome or dangerous I need not be terribly concerned and dwell on the possibility of it occurring, because this will only cause me to unnerve myself.
7. If I don't do perfectly well or even near-perfectly well it's not awful or catastrophic.
8. It's not helpful to fear making mistakes; to do so only creates burdens in living.

9. Doing well is rewarding. Insisting on doing perfectly well only creates unwanted frustration.
10. If I can accept myself regardless of the outcome of any social situation, my fears and apprehensions in this circumstance will lessen greatly.
11. Acceptance of self and ideas by others is nice but not necessary; I can get along nicely without it.
12. Overemphasis on fantasy and striving for materialistic success is much more of a burden than it's worth.
13. Striving for superiority is an unnecessary burden. When I rate others, I create unwanted feelings of jealousy, resentment, anger, and sub- or superhumanness. When I rate myself, I create nonpreferable feelings of shame, guilt, inferiority, and sub- or superhumanness.
14. I don't have to wrestle with or feel guilty about significant others' unhappiness and frustration. I am not responsible for other people's problems and disturbances - nor does this mean I love them any less.
15. Self-consciousness is a very unwanted feeling. It can be effectively dealt with by stubbornly refusing to be overconcerned about what other people might think of me - because in reality it often makes very little difference anyway.
16. Feelings of anxiety, emotional discomfort, strangeness, and nervousness are (a) all part of being human and (b) something I can accept rather than demanding and insisting that the universe make it easier on me by helping me to feel less out of sorts than I sometimes do. It is not necessary to feel at ease at any particular time and when I am not (a) I can stand it, (b) it isn't awful, (c) life will still go on, and (d) I am not less of a person.
17. Feelings of shame, guilt, fear, and anxiety can be minimized by (a) refusing to pass judgment on myself and (b) not dwelling on what others might be thinking about me. People are free to draw their own conclusions about me, and whatever they end up being does in *no way* reflect on me as a human being.
18. I'd best not consider myself to be the one person in the universe who is required to have all the advantages in it. There is no evidence that I have to avoid all life's disadvantages. When I experience these negative happenings, I'd best accept them as keen disappointments and not blow them up into disasters, moan, sulk, whine, or in other ways feel sorry for myself.

Addendum 3

Rational, Nutritional Thoughts As Distinctive from Irrational, Nonnutritional Thoughts

Irrational, nonnutritional thoughts = thoughts that cannot be supported by evidence and in the long run cause you to feel more the way you don't want to feel and less the way you want to feel.

Rational, nutritional thoughts = thoughts that can be supported by evidence and in the long run help you to feel more the way you want to feel and less the way you don't want to feel.

Rational, Nutritional Thinking		As Distinguished From Irrational, Nonnutritional Thinking
1. act	but not	1. overreact
2. involved	but not	2. entangled
3. could have	but not	3. should have
4. emotional	but not	4. emotionalism
5. hassle	but not	5. horror
6. risk taking	but not	6. foolhardy
7. persistent	but not	7. bull-headed
8. wonder	but not	8. worry
9. important	but not	9. all-important
10. important	but not	10. sacred
11. part of life	but not	11. bigger than life

Rational, Nutritional Thinking		**As Distinguished From Irrational, Nonnutritional Thinking**
12. unsure	but not	12. insecure
13. explain	but not	13. overexplain
14. want	but not	14. need
15. prefer	but not	15. demand
16. contentment	but not	16. complacency
17. conscientious	but not	17. perfectionistic
18. want to	but not	18. have to
19. do well	but not	19. perfectly well
20. opinionizing	but not	20. whining
21. better off	but not	21. better person
22. organized	but not	22. compulsive
23. be myself	but not	23. prove myself
24. tell others my feelings	but not	24. tell others off
25. dislike	but not	25. hate
26. unpleasant	but not	26. horrible
27. undelightful	but not	27. awful
28. unhappy	but not	28. sulky
29. examine	but not	29. brood
30. dissatisfied	but not	30. disturbed
31. select against	but not	31. put down
32. criticized	but not	32. insulted
33. regret	but not	33. guilt
34. apprehensive	but not	34. anxious
35. sad	but not	35. depressed
36. annoyed	but not	36. angry
37. hope	but not	37. blind faith
38. questioning	but not	38. nagging
39. self-interest	but not	39. selfish
40. disapproved of	but not	40. discredited
41. confident	but not	41. conceited
42. consistent	but not	42. perfect

Addendum 4

What to Expect from a Rational-Emotive Therapist

Like all humans, RET therapists are not clones of one another. By definition they would all subscribe to the ABCs of emotional re-education. They are most likely to differ in their manner and methods of driving home rational messages. Although some may be more confrontive, direct, or persuasive than others, most are likely to be forthright in quickly teaching you (a) how you upset yourself and, more importantly, (b) what you can actively do to gain better control over your unwanted emotions. If you decide to counsel with an RET therapist come prepared to learn a great deal of information on how to better get along with yourself and others while more fully understanding your previous response to the world around you.

You will likely find empathy but not sympathy; more expectations of you than you have expected of yourself; that you are pushed but not nagged; firm, no-nonsense treatment but much respect. Perhaps more than anything else I respect my clients - the voluntary ones because they have enough guts to admit that they have problems, and the involuntary clients because they have enough sense to know that it is in their best interest to see me, if for no other reason than somebody who has more leverage and authority than they do is insisting on it. In either case, each has a high regard for their own self-interest - which is a good starting point with either clientele.

My bet is that when you meet an RET therapist you will find a teacher who not only thinks differently than you but makes it difficult - by his or her probing, questioning, and active manner of conduct - for you to not respond to him or her. Perhaps the main hallmark of a good teacher is that he or she makes it inviting for his or her students to respond. You are likely to learn more from someone who thinks differently than you - otherwise, discussions likely will be turned into a boring experience. This is what you are least likely to get from an RET therapist - more of the same conventional wisdom that you wrongly believed and that resulted in your emotional concerns to begin with. In short, you are likely to gain that refreshing feeling that comes from new ways of looking at old problems while learning how to overreact less and accept yourself more.

The following description, *About Your Therapy* (pp. 235-239), is a handout I give to each of my clients prior to or following our first session. It is designed to provide clients with a glimpse of RET and to prepare them for their role as client, while explaining many of the things they can expect from and in their therapy. A listing of RET therapists throughout the country and abroad can be ordered from the catalog of the Institute for Rational-Emotive Therapy by writing the Institute at 45 East 65th Street, New York, NY 10021. You may also call the Institute at (212) 535-0822 to request the name of the RET therapist closest to you. If none are available in your locale you can call your local mental health association or clinic, information and referral agency, and/or the help line in your area and ask for names of therapists who practice cognitive and/or cognitive behavior therapy.

Addendum 5

About Your Therapy

To understand and more fully benefit from your therapy it will be important to know and follow these listed points:

1. Your counseling will be educational in nature. Be prepared to learn different ways of thinking and feeling about and acting toward old problems.
2. It will be especially important for you to study and learn the ABCs of emotional reeducation that I will review with you. You largely feel the way you think. You will learn that happenings don't cause feelings but that happenings plus thoughts mainly determine your feelings. This simple understanding will put you more in the driver's seat in better controlling your feelings, because, even though many times you can't influence what events occur in your life, you can control how you think and what you believe about those same occurrences.
3. Readings will be assigned to you. As is true in learning other subjects, it will be important for you to read and study the written material. As you read materials, underline those parts of the writings that you don't understand or have a special interest in for some other reason. Be prepared to discuss these readings with me as part of your therapy. Especially ask yourself about the readings: "What did I learn?" "What did I not understand?" "What idea(s) did I find especially helpful?"
4. Tell others what you're learning about understanding yourself and gaining better control over your life. Teach others who

might be interested in the ABCs of emotional reeducation. One of the best ways to learn something is to teach it!

5. Be active in asking me questions about matters that are important to you. The more questions you ask, the greater likelihood of your profiting from your counseling.
6. Tape our sessions if possible. Clients often report learning more from the playback of their therapy because they can better concentrate then on what was learned in the therapy session. You would be required to supply your own tape.
7. Be sure to understand how assigned and agreed-upon homework will be to your advantage to complete before agreeing to do it.
8. Look for gains within gains and lifelong benefits. The type of therapy that I practice is Rational-Emotive Therapy (RET). One of the ways it is unique is that it is set up to not only help you with the problem you came to me for, but also to assist you with any problem that you presently have or might have in the future. As you begin to change your beliefs about today's concern you probably will find that you can use that changed, more helpful way of thinking with other difficulties.
9. In changing your way of thinking be especially alert for correcting self-statements such as "awful"/"terrible"/"horrible"/"I can't stand it"/"should"/"must"/"have to"/"supposed to"/"ought to"/"need"/"always"/"never"/"every time." These ideas reflect all-or-nothing, black-or-white, absolute-type thinking that promotes emotional upset and disturbance.
10. Be aware that when you are emotionally upset you probably are doing one or both of the following: (a) Overreacting to past, present, or future circumstances by exaggerating the difficulty of something or how bad it is, for example "Isn't it *awful* that. . . ." "Wouldn't it be *terrible* if. . . ." "Wasn't it *horrible* that. . . ." Consistently contrast this way of thinking and you will likely discover a contrast in your feelings, for example, "Isn't it *unfortunate* that. . . ." "Wouldn't it be *regretful* if. . . ." "Wasn't it *disappointing* that. . . ." (b) Self-blaming or self-downing, for example, "I'm a bad person because. . . ." "I am to be damned because. . . ." "I'm no good because. . . ." Try to distinguish between correcting your errors and condemning yourself for making them; between acknowledging and holding yourself accountable and responsible for your shortcomings (including your being unable to get someone to like and approve of you) and damning yourself for having them; between getting after your faults and getting after yourself; and between being disappointed in your flaws and getting

disappointed in you. Take your mistakes seriously, but take yourself lightly. Build a case for self-compassion and self-acceptance. See that you may do stupid things, but that you are not stupid, for example, "I am not a bad person for acting badly," "I have a right to be wrong," "I don't have to discredit or in any way look down on myself for any reason!"

11. Most of what is called emotional upset is a form of demandingness, a protest against reality, a refusal to accept what actually does exist. Frequently that demand or protest comes in the form of the words "should" or "must." There are three basic demands; see if you can detect and track down what yours are for any emotional problem you have. The three core demands that create stress and upset and their counters that help take emotional pressure off yourself are:

a. "*I* must/should/have to be perfect or else I'm perfectly worthless."	→	"There is no evidence that as a human being I have to be perfect - there is proof that I'd like to do well, but that is a far cry from doing perfectly well."
b. "*Others* should/must/have to treat me well with no lapses in kindness and consideration or else they are perfectly worthless."	→	"There is no proof that others are required to treat me pleasantly - and though I would like them to act kindly toward me they definitely have the right to decide this matter for themself."
c. "*Life* should/must/has to be perfectly fair to me and more easily provide me at least some of the advantages I want or else it's rotten and perfectly worthless."	→	"There is no cosmic law that says the universe owes me any special favors - even if I play my cards right and do many of the right things - the universe is not obligated to single me out in giving me what I think I deserve."

12.

Examples of thoughts that cause disturbance		*Examples of contrasting thoughts that help with emotional self-control*
a. "How *awful!*	→	"This is disappointing."

Examples of thoughts that cause disturbance (Continued)		*Examples of contrasting thoughts that help with emotional self-control*
b. "I can't stand it."	→	"I can put up with what I don't like."
c. "I'm stupid."	→	"What I did was stupid."
d. "He stinks!"	→	"He's not perfect either."
e. "This *shouldn't* have happened."	→	"This should have happened because it did!"
f. "I am to be blamed."	→	"I am at fault but am not to be blamed."
g. "She has no right."	→	"She has every right to follow her own mind though I wish she hadn't exercised that right!"
h. "I *need* him/her/that."	→	"I want/desire/prefer him/her/that - but I don't require what I want."
i. "Things *always* go wrong."	→	"Sometimes, if not frequently, things go wrong."
j. "*Every time* I try, I fail."	→	"Sometimes, if not often, I fail."
k. "Things *never* work out."	→	"More often than I would like, things don't work out."
l. "This is bigger than life."	→	"This is an important part of my life, at most."
m. "This *should* be easier."	→	"I wish this were easier, but often things that are good for me aren't - no gain without pain - tough, too bad!"

Examples of thoughts that cause disturbance (Continued)		*Examples of contrasting thoughts that help with emotional self-control*
n. "I *should* have done better."	→	"I would have preferred to do better but instead I did what I could."
o. "I am a failure."	→	"I'm a person who sometimes fails."

13. Read this handout at least several times.

Note. From *You Can Control Your Feelings! 24 Guides to Emotional Well-Being* by Bill Borcherdt.

Bibliography

Alberti, R. E. (1990). *Stand Up, Speak Out, Talk Back.* San Luis Obispo, CA: Impact.

Alberti, R. E., & Emmons, M. L. (1975). *Stand Up, Speak Out, Talk Back!* New York: Pocket Books.

Alberti, R. E., & Emmons, M. L. (1990). *Your Perfect Right: A Guide to Assertive Living* (6th ed.). San Luis Obispo, CA: Impact.

Bach, G. R., & Wyden, P. (1968). *The Intimate Enemy.* New York: Avon.

Becker, W. C. (1971). *Parents Are Teachers.* Champaign, IL: Research Press.

Bell, N. W., & Vogel, E. F. (1965). *The Family.* New York: The Free Press.

Bernard, M. E., & Joyce, M. R. (1984). *Rational-Emotive Therapy with Children and Adolescents.* New York: John Wiley and Sons.

Borcherdt, B. (1989). *Think Straight! Feel Great! 21 Guides to Emotional Self-Control.* Sarasota, FL: Professional Resource Exchange.

Buntman, P. H. (1979). *How to Live with Your Teen-Ager.* Pasadena, CA: The Birch Tree Press.

Dobson, J. (1970). *Dare to Discipline.* New York: Bantam Books.

Dryden, W. (1990). *Dealing with Anger Problems: Rational-Emotive Therapeutic Interventions.* Sarasota, FL: Professional Resource Exchange.

Dryden, W. (1991). *A Dialogue with Albert Ellis: Against Dogma.* Philadelphia, PA: Open University Press.

Dryden, W., & DiGiuseppe, R. (1990). *A Primer on Rational-Emotive Therapy.* San Jose, CA: Resource Press.

Dryden, W., & Golden, W. L. (1987). *Cognitive-Behavioral Approaches to Psychotherapy.* Bristol, PA: Hemisphere Publishing.

Ellis, A. (1961). *A Guide to a Successful Marriage.* N. Hollywood, CA: Wilshire Book Company.

Ellis, A. (1965). *Suppressed: 7 Key Essays Publishers Dared Not Print.* Chicago, IL: New Classics House.

Ellis, A. (1966a). *The Art and Science of Love.* Secaucus, NJ: Lyle Stuart.

Ellis, A. (1966b). *How to Raise an Emotionally Healthy, Happy Child.* N. Hollywood, CA: Wilshire Book Company.

Ellis, A. (1971). *Growth Through Reason.* N. Hollywood, CA: Wilshire Book Company.

Ellis, A. (1972a). *The Civilized Couples Guide to Extra-Marital Affairs.* New York: Peter H. Wyden.

Ellis, A. (1972b). *The Sensuous Person: Critique and Corrections.* Secaucus, NJ: Lyle Stuart.

Ellis, A. (1974). *Humanistic Psychotherapy.* New York: McGraw-Hill.

Ellis, A. (1975). *How to Live with a Neurotic at Home and Work.* New York: Crown Publishers.

Ellis, A. (1979a). *The Intelligent Woman's Guide to Dating and Mating.* Secaucus, NJ: Lyle Stuart.

Ellis, A. (1979b). *Overcoming Procrastination.* New York: Signet.

Ellis, A. (1979c). *Reason and Emotion in Psychotherapy.* Secaucus, NJ: The Citadel Press.

Ellis, A. (1982). *Rational Assertiveness Training* (Audiotape). New York: Institute for Rational Living.

Ellis, A. (1988). *How to Stubbornly Refuse to Make Yourself Miserable About Anything--Yes, Anything!* Secaucus, NJ: Lyle Stuart.

Ellis, A. (1991). *Why Am I Always Broke: How to be Sure about Money*. New York: Carol Publishing.

Ellis, A. (1992). *When AA Doesn't Work for You: A Rational Guide to Quitting Alcohol*. Barricade Books.

Ellis, A., & Abrahms, E. (1978). *Brief Psychotherapy in Medical and Health Practice*. New York: Springer.

Ellis, A., & Becker, I. (1982). *A Guide to Personal Happiness*. N. Hollywood, CA: Wilshire Book Company.

Ellis, A., & Harper, R. (1975). *A New Guide to Rational Living*. N. Hollywood, CA: Wilshire Book Company.

Ellis, A., & Whiteley, J. (1979). *Theoretical and Empirical Foundation of Rational-Emotive Therapy*. Monterey, CA: Brooks/Cole.

Ellis, A., & Yeager, R. J. (1989). *Why Some Therapies Don't Work: The Dangers of Transpersonal Psychology*. Buffalo, NY: Prometheus Books.

Fensterheim, H., & Baer, J. (1977). *Don't Say Yes When You Want to Say No*. New York: Dell.

Fraiberg, S. H. (1959). *The Magic Years*. New York: Charles Scribner's Sons.

Frankl, V. E. (1959). *Man's Search for Meaning*. New York: Touchstone Books.

Garcia, E. (1979). *Developing Emotional Muscle*. Atlanta: Author.

Garner, A. (1981). *Conversationally Speaking*. New York: McGraw-Hill.

Glasser, W. (1975). *Reality Therapy*. New York: Harper Colophon Books.

Greenberg, D. (1966). *How to Make Yourself Miserable*. New York: Random House.

Greiger, R. M., & Boyd, J. D. (1980). *Rational-Emotive Therapy: A Skills Based Approach*. New York: Van Nostrand Reinhold.

Grossack, M. (1976). *Love, Sex, and Self-Fulfillment*. New York: Signet.

Haley, J., & Hoffman, L. (1967). *Techniques of Family Therapy*. New York: Basic Books.

Harris, S. (1982). *Pieces of Eight*. Boston: Houghton Mifflin.

Hauck, P. (1971). *Marriage Is a Loving Business.* Philadelphia, PA: The Westminster Press.

Hauck, P. (1974). *Overcoming Frustration and Anger.* Philadelphia, PA: The Westminster Press.

Hauck, P. (1976). *How to Do What You Want to Do.* Philadelphia, PA: The Westminster Press.

Hauck, P. (1978). *Overcoming Depression.* Philadelphia, PA: The Westminster Press.

Hauck, P. (1981). *Overcoming Jealousy and Possessiveness.* Philadelphia, PA: The Westminster Press.

Hauck, P. (1984). *The Three Faces of Love.* Philadelphia, PA: The Westminster Press.

Hoffer, E. (1966). *The True Believer.* New York: Perennial Library.

Holt, J. (1970a). *How Children Fail.* New York: Dell.

Holt, J. (1970b). *How Children Learn.* New York: Dell.

James, M., & Jongeward, D. (1973). *Born to Win.* Reading, PA: Addison-Wesley.

Johnson, W. R. (1981). *So Desperate the Fight.* New York: Institute for Rational Living.

Jourard, S. (1971). *The Transparent Self.* New York: D. Van Nostrand.

Lazarus, A. A. (1981). *The Practice of Multi-Modal Therapy.* New York: McGraw-Hill.

Lazarus, A. A. (1984). *In the Minds Eye: The Power of Imagery for Personal Enrichment.* New York: Guilford.

Lazarus, A. A. (1985). *Marital Myths: Two Dozen Mistaken Beliefs That Can Ruin a Marriage (or Make a Bad One Worse).* San Luis Obispo, CA: Impact.

Lazarus, A. A. (1989). *The Practice of Multimodal Therapy: Systematic, Comprehensive and Effective Psychotherapy.* Johns Hopkins.

Lazarus, A. A., & Fay, A. (1975). *I Can if I Want to.* New York: Warner Books.

Maultsby, M. (1975). *Help Yourself to Happiness.* New York: Institute for Rational Living.

Meichenbaum, D. (1977). *Cognitive-Behavior Modification: An Integrative Approach.* New York: Plenum.

Paris, C., & Casey, B. (1979). *Project: You, a Manual of Rational Assertiveness Training.* Portland, OR: Bridges Press.

Paterson, G. R. (1978). *Families*. Champaign, IL: Research Press.

Perls, F. S. (1969). *In and Out of the Garbage Pail.* New York: Bantam Books.

Putney, S., & Putney, G. J. (1966). *The Adjusted American: Normal Neuroses in the Individual and Society.* New York: Harper Colophon Books.

Reisman, D. (1962). *The Lonely Crowd.* New Haven: Yale University Press.

Russell, B. (1971). *The Conquest of Happiness*. New York: Liveright.

Russianoff, P. (1983). *Why Do I Think I'm Nothing Without a Man?* New York: Bantam Books.

Satir, V. (1967). *Conjoint Family Therapy.* Palo Alto, CA: Science and Behavior Books.

Satir, V. (1972). *Peoplemaking.* Palo Alto, CA: Science and Behavior Books.

Shedd, C. W. (1978). *Smart Dads I Know.* New York: Avon.

Simon, S. B. (1978). *Negative Criticism and What You Can Do About It.* Niles, IL: Argus Communications.

Smith, M. J. (1975). *When I Say No, I Feel Guilty.* New York: Bantam Books.

Walen, S. R., DiGiuseppe, R., & Wessler, R. L. (1980). *A Practitioner's Guide to Rational-Emotive Therapy.* New York: Oxford University Press.

Weeks, C. (1981). *Simple, Effective Treatment of Agoraphobia.* New York: Bantam Books.

Young, H. S. (1974). *A Rational Counseling Primer.* New York: Institute for Rational Living.

Zilbergeld, B. (1978). *Male Sexuality.* Boston, MA: Little, Brown, and Company.

Zilbergeld, B. (1983). *The Shrinking of America: Myths of Psychological Change.* Boston, MA: Little, Brown, and Company.

Zilbergeld, B. (1992). *The New Male Sexuality.* New York: Bantam Books.

Zilbergeld, B., & Lazarus, A. A. (1988). *Mindpower: Getting What You Want Through Mental Training.* New York: Ivy Books.

If You Found This Book Useful . . .

You might want to know more about our other titles.

If you would like to receive our latest catalog, please return this form:

Name:____
(Please Print)

Address:____

Address:____

City/State/Zip:______________________________________

Telephone:(__________)______________________________

I am a:

_________ Psychologist
_________ Psychiatrist
_________ School Psychologist
_________ Clinical Social Worker
_________ Mental Health Counselor
_________ Marriage and Family Therapist
_________ Not in Mental Health Field
_________ Other:__________________

◆ ◆ ◆

Professional Resource Press
P.O. Box 15560
Sarasota, FL 34277-1560

Telephone #941-366-7913
FAX #941-366-7971